THE

LEARN YOUR VALUE.

WORTHY

OWN IT.

PROJECT

CELEBRATE IT.

MEADOW DeVOR

Copyright © 2021, 2022 by Meadow DeVor
Cover and internal design © 2022 by Sourcebooks
Cover design by Jillian Rahn/Sourcebooks
Cover images © Mark Windom/Stocksy United, bosotochka/Getty Images
Internal design by Michelle Mayhall/Sourcebooks

This publication is designed to provide accurate and authoritative information
in regard to the subject matter covered. It is sold with the understanding
that the publisher is not engaged in rendering legal, accounting, or other
professional service. If legal advice or other expert assistance is required,
the services of a competent professional person should be sought. —*From
a Declaration of Principles Jointly Adopted by a Committee of the American
Bar Association and a Committee of Publishers and Associations*

Published by Sourcebooks
P.O. Box 4410, Naperville, Illinois 60567-4410
(630) 961-3900
sourcebooks.com

Originally published in audiobook format in 2021 in the United
States by Audible Originals, an imprint of Audible, Inc.

Cataloging-in-Publication Data is on file with the Library of Congress.

Printed and bound in the United States of America.
VP 10 9 8 7 6 5 4 3 2 1

To Blake

Contents

Introduction

What if I told you the quality of every single aspect of your life—your relationships, your bank accounts, your home, your emotional health—boils down to one thing?

This one thing? An unwavering understanding of your own immeasurable value. This understanding is at the core of how you see yourself and how you allow the world to see you. It is what I call *worth*.

Self-worth, worthy, worthiness... These words are tricky. You know that you're supposed to value yourself, but what does it actually mean to cultivate self-worth, and how do you do it?

Worthiness is the quality of deserving attention, energy, and respect. It's not confidence. It's not bravado. You can't fake worthiness, nor can you accidentally end up with it.

> *Worthiness is the quality of deserving attention, energy, and respect. You can't fake worthiness, nor can you accidentally end up with it.*

Worthiness is like a muscle. There are things you can do to strengthen that muscle, and there are plenty of things that will weaken it. Think of worthiness as a strong backbone with a soft heart. The backbone is held strong by dozens of muscles working together. Their strength holds you, protects you, and gives you support. The soft heart allows vulnerability, intimacy, and authenticity to shine through.

Worthiness will not be granted to you, bestowed upon you, or awarded to you. No amount of money, fame, or success will ever be able to deem you worthy. Worthiness can't be found in IQ points, in fancy degrees, or by winning gold medals. Because worthiness is an inside job.

I am here today to tell you how to do the job right. I'm going to show you how to stop undervaluing yourself, how to stop giving yourself away for cheap, and how to start investing in yourself. I'll help you understand the concept of self-worth and how it affects every aspect of your life. I'll help you evaluate your own self-worth and identify the unexpected ways in which your lack of self-worth may be keeping you from what you deserve. And I'll give you unexpected, actionable steps to help you put these concepts to work right away.

Take a minute to look around you. Take a snapshot of your life as it is, right here, right now. Peppered throughout your life, you'll see evidence of what you believe you're worth. Maybe you can never seem to get that promotion at work, or you're stuck living paycheck to paycheck, or you have a difficult time telling people no. Maybe you never quite get around to fixing that broken faucet. Maybe you can't figure out how to get your kids, your aunt Hilda, or that perky PTA president to take you seriously. These issues might seem unrelated, but they are all symptoms of the same underlying problem: a lack of self-worth.

To live as if you are worthy means to be connected to this world, to your life, and to yourself. This means that every part of your life—your finances, your boundaries, your relationships, how you keep your home, what you wear—receives attention and respect. It means that you begin to deal with the leaky faucet, or you initiate a difficult conversation with Aunt Hilda. It means that you make a small attempt to use your voice or that you take a baby step toward bettering your relationship with money.

In *The Worthy Project*, through a six-week practice of small, deliberate changes in behavior, you will begin to clarify what strengthens or weakens your sense of self-worth and how to reinforce your worthiness through daily actions and routines.

> *To live as if you are worthy means to be connected to this world, to your life, and to yourself.*

Worthiness can be learned and it can be practiced. You can learn how to live the full expression of life. You can learn how to live with an unwavering understanding of your own immeasurable value. You can actually learn to own your worth.

◊ ◊ ◊

Today, I live with an abiding sense of worthiness—a strong backbone and a soft heart—but I didn't always feel this way. If you took a snapshot of my life in 2009, you'd see evidence of weak self-worth scattered throughout the rubble of my recent divorce. You'd see it in my lack of boundaries and in the people I surrounded myself with. It was obvious in the way I parented and how guilty I felt most nights as I went to bed. You'd see it in the way I felt alone and in my failed attempts to fill that aloneness.

But most of all, you'd see it in my finances.

In 2009, my real estate assets, my personal coaching business, and a few hundred thousand dollars owed to me all vaporized, seemingly overnight. Before that point, I had owned two homes; I had been working as a life coach—primarily making my living from private coaching sessions, teaching online courses, leading in-person trainings, and hosting weekend retreats; and I had been receiving monthly payments for a music school that I'd previously owned and sold. Over the course of a few months, real estate values plummeted, business dried up, and the person who had bought my previous business was unable to continue making payments. These three simultaneous events left me with $571,817.68 of debt. Up until that point, I'd never thought of myself as being in real financial trouble. In January of that year, I'd believed that I was just experiencing a post-divorce low. My plan had been to spend a month or so licking my wounds, then get back to work, to start producing income. I thought everything would be okay. By July, I realized—too late—how very wrong I'd been.

For most of my life, I had secretly felt worthless, unlovable, and unwanted, and I didn't know how to deal with those debilitating feelings. Before my financial life came crashing down, I tried to create worthiness on the outside of me, not knowing that by doing so, I was actually reinforcing my lack of self-worth. I bought things I thought would stave off the feelings of failure, of not being enough. I paid for things that would keep people from seeing the real me, the tragically flawed and unworthy person who I believed myself to be. In the first half of 2009—a time when I was in critical financial trouble and should have been watching every penny—I booked myself a trip to Europe to visit a friend so I'd feel less alone. I also spent a small fortune on clothes and completely refurnished my little post-divorce home, thinking that new furniture would make me feel more successful.

I didn't know that my self-worth was deteriorating with each of these decisions. I had no idea what worthiness really meant.

Between all this United MileagePlus card–sponsored jet-setting and clothes shopping and home decorating, I barely noticed the tumbleweeds blowing through my calendar. What was once a robust client lineup had disappeared. No appointments. No clients. No classes or trainings. Just long columns of white space on my calendar.

Before 2009, I'd had success in my coaching career. I'd worked for Martha Beck, one of the leading women in the self-development industry. I was a guest on *The Oprah Winfrey Show*. I'd become accustomed to my classes selling out immediately and to ever-growing wait lists for my private clients. Before 2009, I had plenty of time, energy, and attention to give my business. I didn't worry about how well my next offering would sell. Ironically, most of my income had come from teaching new coaches how to make six figures in the first year of launching their businesses. My coaching tools and strategies were strong, and they worked, but they only applied to a narrow aspect of money: earning potential. At that point, I didn't address spending or debt, nor did I understand how deeply one's unconscious sense of worthiness affects their relationship to money, to love, or to life itself. Combining my blind optimism and my hard work ethic, I simply taught others to do what I had done. Work hard. Make money. I was known as the "money girl." To me, money was easy.

Or so I thought.

As I struggled to care for my six-year-old daughter and repair my life post-divorce, I didn't have the bandwidth to market myself, go on speaking tours, or do what it took to keep a consistent client base in a spiraling economy. Nor could I understand then how deeply the self-development industry had been hit by the recession. I didn't know what to do with my newly empty calendar. I told myself that it was just a blip, that the students would start filing in again, that this was just a temporary setback. I paced a lot. I started checking my email more frequently. Refresh, nothing. Refresh, still nothing.

Given these hard facts, it's hard to explain how I could continue with my blindly optimistic outlook. The truth is, I wasn't looking at the facts. Instead, I tried my hardest *not* to look at them. I believed that if I kept my mind squarely set on positivity, my life would work itself out. I didn't see that the failed marriage, the failing career, the mountains of debt, and my terrible feeling of being a fraud, an impostor, a loser were all symptoms of the same problem. I didn't see that every action I took actually made my problem bigger.

> I believed that if I kept my mind squarely set on positivity, my life would work itself out.

I'd already lost my ass in the real estate market. My business was tanking. And in July 2009, the money owed to me from the sale of my previous business—hundreds of thousands of dollars—evaporated in the span of a phone call.

That phone call is where my memory goes blank. I don't remember if I spoke, if I hung up the phone, or if I cried. I don't remember just how long it took me to understand what the phone call meant. I'd been so committed to my fantasies and my it's-all-going-to-be-okay belief system that I don't actually remember if the facade cracked open and immediately lay in rubble at my feet or if there was a longer process of painfully peeling myself out of the artificial image that had once been my life. I'm thinking that it must have been the slower one, the more painful one.

Up until that phone call, I believed that everything was going to be okay. It was going to be okay that I went to Europe and put the whole thing on my Visa Platinum card. It was going to be okay that I'd squandered a few thousand bucks on a Gucci dress for no legitimate reason other than to impress some women who barely knew me. And that I only wore said Gucci dress twice before it was ruined at a wedding by a drunk lady with a rogue glass of red wine. It was going to be okay that I'd given away an entire house of furniture and practically bought the entire Pottery Barn catalog (sponsored by Visa) to replace it all. It was going to be okay that my calendar was barren and the high point of my career might have been behind me. It was going to be okay that I lost my home and all my money. It was going to be okay that my marriage was over and that the divorce had uprooted my daughter's life. It was going to be okay that I owed hundreds of thousands of dollars. It was all going to be okay, because I had a payment coming to me. That was how I thought my story was going to end: a big, fat check made out to Happily Ever After.

Except that's not what happened.

After that phone call, stunned and confused, I tried to make sense of the events of my life. I'd been a good person and followed all the rules. I'd always been a hard worker with high credit scores who paid my bills on time. Sure, I had made some reckless purchases in the past year, but that couldn't have been why I was here, circling this drain of misfortune. It couldn't have been *my* fault. I spent a good stint of time blaming others—it was the government's fault, my real estate agent's fault, the banking system's fault, my ex-husband's fault.

But my pity party didn't last long because, truth be told, self-pity is expensive, and I just couldn't afford the indulgence. I'd come to a place where there was no more room on the cards, there were no more lines of credit to rely on, I could no longer rob Peter to pay Paul, and I could no longer cover even the minimum payments on the balances I'd accrued. I had almost no income, and it was time to come to terms with reality: the bills weren't going to go away, I was the one who had to pay them, and no one was coming to save me.

This was my rock bottom—the place where I had no other choice than to start telling the truth—and the truth wasn't pretty. In fact, it was terrifying. I made a list of what I owed. I made a list of things I could sell. I started dealing with the cold, hard facts of what I was facing. I took an inventory of what had become my life and finally asked myself a different question, a question that changed everything: *What is my part in this?*

> *I took an inventory of what had become my life and finally asked myself a different question: What is my part in this?*

This question opened up a new world to me, a world where I could see that my coaching career might be failing because—who woulda thought—maybe unhappy life coaches weren't really trending in this particular market. Maybe I had made some not-so-great real estate decisions; perhaps renting would have been smarter than buying a home at the top of the market. Maybe I should have cut up my credit cards long ago. Maybe spending money based on a fantasy future isn't the hallmark of financial intelligence. Maybe an unsecured loan isn't something to completely rely on for bailout, because if things went badly (and they did), I'd be the one holding nothing but meaningless paper with no way to recoup the money owed to me.

Underneath all these symptoms was a glaring problem that I couldn't yet articulate. There was a pattern of financial decisions based on what I'd hoped for rather than on what reality had actually presented. I had overestimated the positive possibilities and underestimated what might go wrong. My behaviors hadn't been based on who I was at the time but rather on who I'd imagined I'd become someday. I fixed my sights on my hopeful success story and did my best to ignore the darker truth: that I felt hollow and worthless and had attempted to solve this feeling by being reckless with my resources and idealistic about the future. I had thought that worthiness was something I could attain, buy, or even fake. I'd thought that if I was pretty enough, skinny enough, married enough, success-ful enough, I'd elude the terrible feelings of worthlessness and shame that permeated my inner life. When my financial facade came tumbling down, I was left with nothing but myself and the devastating feelings that I'd failed to outrun.

> **My behaviors hadn't been based on who I was at the time but rather on who I'd imagined I'd become someday.**

I was a thirty-five-year-old single mother. I had no money left, almost no career to speak of, and a gigantic pile of debt. I racked my brain to think of quick and easy solutions. I consid-ered starting a new business. I considered going back to school and starting over with a new career—maybe graphic design or getting my teaching credential. I kept grasping at hopeful ideas, but they wouldn't stick because all these options required two things that I didn't have: time and money. No matter which way I looked at it, there would be no quick or easy fix.

The unthinkable thing was to continue being a coach. I had built my small empire on being the "money girl," and now I was flat broke. I'd be nothing but a sham, a charlatan, a fraud, a liar. I wanted to delete myself from the world (and the internet) until I was fixed, not so broken, not so defective. But there was nowhere to hide, no plan B, and no bailout available.

From my newfound rock-bottom truth-telling place, I could see that no matter what I chose to do, it was going to be hard, and it was going to take time. At that point, I'd already spent five years in the self-development industry. My career wasn't just a profession for me; it was a deeply meaningful calling. I'd spent five years not only teaching but living and breathing the tools that had radically changed my life and the lives of hundreds of my students.

Even in my early coaching years, my work stood on a foundation of self-inquiry tools that pulled from cognitive, emotional, physical, and spiritual practices. Those tools were powerful, and I used them daily. I knew that the decision to continue as a coach came down to choosing to shelter my precious ego or cast myself into the fiery crucible of spiritual growth. I had a hunch that the challenge—trying to understand emotionally, financially, and spiritually why I landed in this place—would become the work of my life. Although reinvention seemed sexier, I ultimately knew which path I had to take: the one that terrified me, the one that could possibly ruin what was left of my career, the one that might ultimately set me free.

In early 2010, I held my breath and pushed Publish on my first money blog post that began a truthful conversation between me and my readers. I shared openly about my personal finances. I expected radio silence or a mass exodus of people unsubscribing from my newsletter, but to my surprise, that's not what happened. Instead I got floods of emails saying "Me too," "Thank you for your courage," and "Please keep writing. I'm so glad I'm not the only one." Apparently, lots of people had failed in their attempt to live the American dream.

I had a lot of questions and no good answers, so I asked my readers if they wanted to help me do some research. I was no longer interested in solely looking at the income side of money. Rather, I was intrigued by people's relationships with money. I wanted to look at these relationships in the same way I'd look at any intimate relationship, to have deeper conversations about money and learn everything I could about emotionality as it pertained to what people have in their bank accounts.

I began offering inexpensive coaching packages focused on helping my clients better understand their relationships with money. Trends started to appear as I spent thousands of hours coaching through innumerable daily emails. These emails detailed my clients' financial transactions as well as their innermost thoughts and feelings. Through this research, I developed a new way to teach and coach about money. For the next decade, I taught clients how to stop their compulsive spending, how to pay off their debts, and how to connect the dots between day-to-day transactions and overall net worth.

Yet money is only one aspect of life, and over time, it

became clear that there was a deeper issue that still hadn't been addressed. Whether it was someone's financial net worth, the depth of intimacy felt in their relationships, or their ability to find happiness and well-being, progress only happened up to a point. Then, it was as if they had a self-imposed ceiling where growth no longer seemed possible.

I had come up against that ceiling too. Even though I'd paid off my debt, the nagging feeling of worthlessness still haunted me. I'd radically improved my relationship with money, but I hadn't healed my underlying problem: nonexistent self-worth. I became a workaholic, I continued settling for less than I deserved, and I still had problematic boundary issues. I still lived with daily mom shame and debilitating body shame. For years, my low ceiling of worthiness kept me small, feeling shitty about myself, and stuck.

It wasn't until I began to look at building self-worth in the same way that I looked at building financial net worth that something clicked. I knew how to build net worth: spend less than you earn. I began looking at my porous boundaries, my lack of backbone, the ways I gave myself away for cheap, and my crippling shame through the same lens as a spending problem. I began looking at my time, my energy, and my vitality as something that I could save, like a savings account, but rather than building wealth, I'd be investing in self-worth. I applied this newfound approach to my own life. I stopped spending my energy in ways that reinforced a sense of worthlessness and began saving that energy only for things that strengthened my sense of worthiness. I began sleeping more instead of sacrificing my need for rest. I repainted my furniture bright white rather than settling for old muddy brown. I stopped mindlessly piling my laundry on the floor and organized my closet. I bought food that I loved and stopped worrying about trying to be thin. I silenced my phone notifications and cozied up for nightly TV time with my daughter. For the first time in my life, I began to feel, act, and live with a deep sense of worthiness. Since then, I've taught hundreds of students to do the same.

> I began looking at my time, my energy, and my vitality as something that I could save, like a savings account, but rather than building wealth, I'd be investing in self-worth.

I designed the Worthy Project to sneak in through the back door of your consciousness, looking for the clues about the status of your self-worth that are all around you rather than tackling your dysfunctional thought patterns and feelings head-on. Instead of trying to sift through what you already know about yourself, you'll look for hints in the evidence your

life provides. It's almost impossible to do deep and meaningful inner work when you're really struggling. So throughout
this project, I'll share practical guidelines and action steps that
can be put into practice immediately—what I call *worthy work*.
These action steps will teach you how to feel, act, and live as
if you are worthy. Some of these action steps will appear to be
completely off topic (they're not). You'll look at where you overspend and overgive. You'll look at where you put yourself into
emotional debt, sell yourself short, and chip away at your self-
worth. You'll look at where you underearn and under-receive,
not only at work but also in your closest relationships. You'll
focus on unexpected, easy-to-understand things like your
refrigerator, your junk drawer, or your hallway closet. You'll
be a detective looking for clues—the secret ways that you've
undermined your own sense of self-worth and unknowingly
sabotaged your worthiness.

The Worthy Project is about choosing between two
cycles: the worthy cycle and the worthless cycle. When you're
in the worthy cycle, your behavior reinforces your belief that
you are worth your time and attention. When you're in the
worthless cycle, your behavior reinforces your belief that
you're not worth your own time and attention. The Worthy
Project is about looking at specific aspects of your life (like
the doormat on your front doorstep, your next meal, or the
inside of your handbag) to determine whether these things
reinforce a sense of worthiness or whether they reinforce a
sense of worthlessness in your life. To build self-worth, you
need to spend more time in the worthy cycle than in the

worthless cycle. To live life in the worthy cycle, you need to change your behavior. This doesn't mean that you have to change in huge ways. Rather, you sweep your doorstep, or you sit down at a table for a meal, or you archive all that junk in your inbox. You do small things to teach yourself that you are worth attention and respect.

> "The Worthy Project is about choosing between two cycles: the worthy cycle and the worthless cycle."

Before we begin to take action, let's start with a very nonscientific quiz. The intention of this quiz is to simply offer you a rough idea of your starting point. Please keep in mind: there's no such thing as a perfect sense of self-worth, nor is there any way to measure it. Worthiness isn't a simple on-off switch; it's a complex quality that can be strengthened over time through deliberate practice. As you learn to strengthen your sense of self-worth and begin to put the tools found here into action, you'll be amazed at how quickly your sense of self-worth can change. So the intention of this self-assessment is to take a quick snapshot of who you are before you begin your worthy work so that you can look back and see your progress at the end.

WORTHINESS QUIZ

True or false:
1. I tend to take things personally.
2. I often feel self-conscious in social situations.
3. I have unhealthy/harmful habits that I wish I could break.
4. I probably care too much about what other people think.
5. I feel insecure about how I look.
6. I feel like I'm not good enough (smart enough or capable enough) to achieve what I want to in life.
7. I'm afraid that I am innately flawed.
8. I often settle for less than I probably deserve.
9. I don't believe I can really have what I want.
10. I compare myself to others on social media and feel like I'm not keeping up.
11. I'm not reaching my goals because I give up too soon.
12. If people really knew me, they probably wouldn't like me.
13. I'm often exhausted at the end of the day and feel like I can never do enough for those around me.
14. I have a difficult time saying no.
15. I would say I am a people pleaser.
16. I have a difficult time asking for help.
17. I often feel like others have their lives more together than I do.
18. I apologize, even when I haven't done anything wrong.
19. I often put other people's well-being before my own.
20. I feel uncomfortable receiving gifts, compliments, or favors from others.

Total True _____. Total False _____.

- ◊ 0 True: You are a unicorn and you can put the book down now—you're done! This level of self-worth is almost never found in the wild. You are a mysterious and magical creature, and even though I've never met one of your kind, I do hope you exist.
- ◊ 1–5 True: High five! You feel pretty damned good about yourself (yay, you!), and there are just a couple of places where you feel a bit limited. As you move through this work, focus on the aspects of life where you feel more insecure.
- ◊ 6–15 True: You're not alone. In fact, you're the most common among us. You're a kind and compassionate person, and you simply need some better tools. You're in the right place! Go through this book and do the exercises. You'll be amazed at how quickly and easily this works.
- ◊ 16–20 True: I see you. I get you. And I have nothing but love for you. I created this quiz from my own experience. I lived with the weight and pain of believing every single one of these ideas. Once upon a time, I would have marked all twenty true. Nowadays, I'm damned near unicorn status. Even though you might think this work is insurmountable, you have the most to gain. You can do this.

CHAPTER 1

Worthy and Worthless Cycles

Worth is a word that gets tossed around often, but what does it really mean? Before we start digging into ways of building self-worth, we need to start with a basic understanding of the concept of worth. The simplest way to demonstrate worth is to talk about money. Once you understand how worth works in relation to money, it's pretty simple to start viewing self-worth as a kind of personal bank account.

Let's start with two different women as examples. The first, Lisa, uses shopping to cope with stress and fritters away her money through mindless spending—a T-shirt from Marshalls, a new book from Amazon, a pair of sandals from Zappos. Lisa is a hard worker, but she never asks for a raise. She's terrified of losing her job and doesn't want to rock the boat. She's barely living paycheck to paycheck. She works hard and asks for little in return, thinking that by doing so, she'll be more valuable to the company. This backfires: too much Lisa and too little demand for her doesn't make her more valuable. In fact, it does the opposite—it cheapens her value. When bonus time comes along, Lisa is skipped over.

Lisa overspends and underearns. Over time, she goes deeper into debt.

The other woman, Jessica, is very careful with her money. She's conscious and deliberate about her spending and only pays for things that she truly values. Rather than having a bunch of meaningless stuff, she prefers to keep her money in the bank. She always spends less than she earns and saves the rest. Jessica knows that her work is valuable to the company. She has a nice cushion of savings and feels confident asking for a raise. She knows that her skills are highly marketable, trusts that she'd easily find another job, and understands that very few would be able to fill her shoes. Her boss knows this too and quickly agrees to increase her salary.

Jessica is a conscious spender and a strong earner. Over time, she builds wealth.

Even if you're not a financial wizard, it should be easy to determine who ends up with more financial worth. Financial worth increases with Jessica's strategy. Financial worth tanks with Lisa's strategy.

Now, let's look at these same two women from a different perspective.

Lisa doesn't have a strong sense of *self*. She doesn't really know who she is, and she doesn't really know what she wants. Her focus on others eclipses her inner sense of self. She relieves her restlessness, her feeling of not-enough-ness, by offering more of herself to those around her. She gives herself away to her neighbors, to her friends, and to her family. Because she gives so much of herself without asking for anything in return, her life fills with people who don't really respect her and people who don't truly care about her. Over time, she gives more of herself away than she keeps. Lisa ends up becoming less and less of who she really is—less of her*self.*

Jessica, on the other hand, has a pretty strong sense of self. Just like with her money, she's careful with how she spends her time, her attention, and her energy. She doesn't give away more of herself than she can afford. Because she's careful with her generosity and deliberate with what she requires in return, her life is filled with people who respect her and truly care for her. Over time, she keeps more of herself than she gives away. Jessica ends up becoming more and more of who she really is— more of her own self.

WHAT IS WORTH?

When I lost everything in the Great Recession, I definitely wasn't alone. Hundreds of thousands of people watched their livelihoods, investments, and life savings dwindle down to almost nothing. According to an NPR article published five years after the crisis, American households alone lost sixteen trillion dollars. At the time, I'd get frustrated hearing stats like that. I'd thought that money was a zero-sum game, meaning the gains and losses always needed to balance out, so I'd try to imagine where that sixteen trillion went. If we lost it, who found it?

To answer that question, let's start by tracing out where my own tiny sliver of the sixteen trillion went.

Prerecession, most of my money was held in real estate assets. I'd invested a lot of money and years of my life into these assets, and they'd become a nice little nest egg. By the time I filed for divorce and needed to sell my real estate holdings, the housing market was in the middle of collapsing on itself, and my investments were what they call "upside down," meaning that rather than having a nice nest egg, I had a big chunk of debt. But when I look at the source of the loss, I can't say that anyone stole my money, nor can I say that I gave it to anyone. In one moment, I was worth a certain amount of money, and then the next, I was worth a radically lower amount of money.

In the realm of money, worth follows a basic supply and demand model. Money is traded for things. To build financial worth, you must keep more of that value than you spend. If things become too easy to get, value collapses and worth vanishes.

This is also how self-worth works. To build self-worth, you must keep more value than you spend. Where financial worth is the accumulation of a thing called *money*, self-worth is the accumulation of a thing called *self*.

To build self-worth, you must keep more value than you spend.

YOUR TRUE SELF

Just like money, *self* can be earned, and it can be spent. It can be saved, and it can be invested. It can be used as a type of currency. Its value can be determined by supply and demand. And you build worth, specifically *self*-worth, by accumulating more *self*. In other words, to raise your self-worth, you must claim, own, and possess more of your *self*.

Let's call this aspect of self your *true self*. Your true self is what distinguishes you from anyone else. It's your essence, your true nature. It's the you-ness that makes you *you*. Your *true self* is the authentic, central, and essential part of who you are. The real you that exists in your human body, right here, right now. This is the you that has the ability to dream and create. It is the you that's able to be in relationships with others—the you that has the capacity to love, feel, explore, think, decide, and create throughout your life. This is the most vulnerable part of you, the part that you must protect, the part you must invest in.

The true self is your most valuable asset, and by honoring, respecting, and caring for your true self, you change the tide of supply and demand of *self*. By stewarding the true self, value increases and self-worth builds. This means that to feel, act, and live with an abiding sense of worthiness, your awareness must start with your true self.

When you lose your sense of *true self* or you give too much of yourself to a person, a cause, or a role, you experience a real and painful loss that feels like not-enough-ness—the source of unworthiness. You sense the diminishment of self, and you

> *The true self is your most valuable asset, and by honoring, respecting, and caring for your true self, you change the tide of supply and demand of self.*

experience the pain of being less than. But in reality, you don't cut off a finger and give it to a guy you like in hopes that he likes you back—at least I hope you don't. Rather, you may give up an intangible piece of who you really are—like saying, *Oh, you love death metal? Me too!*—in hopes that you're more attractive as a less-you version of your*self*. And by being reckless with this precious asset of *true self*, your worth declines.

Just like with any currency, you build self-worth by keeping more than you give away. And if you compulsively overspend or habitually underearn, you'll eventually run into serious problems. In the realm of money, this rock-bottom place is called bankruptcy. In the realm of self-worth, rock bottom is a sense of worthlessness.

It's important to understand that you alone are the determiner of the supply and demand of *true self*. You are the spender, the earner, the investor. This means that you are the only one who can determine, influence, or change your worth.

> *You alone are the determiner of the supply and demand of true self.*

This is great news because no matter how emotionally bankrupt you feel, there is a way out. By changing your strategy from worth depleting to worth building, you'll begin to see your rare and precious *true self* as a valuable asset worth investing in.

TRUE SELF VS. IDEAL IMAGE

To change your strategy to worth building, you must first understand the difference between your true self and your *ideal image*. Your *ideal image* is the social role or identity that you want to attain, cultivate, or portray to others. It's the way you want to be seen by yourself and by those around you. It's the socialized identity that family, friends, community, marketing, and society at large has taught you to value. The ideal image doesn't live in your human body, right here, right now. Rather, it's a romanticized fantasy that exists only in your imagination. It's not an aspect of your true self; rather it's the ever-changing illusion of who you think you should be, what you think you should have, or what you think you should do. This ideal image is concerned with exterior, superficial, and other-centric concepts.

At first glance, it may seem like the ideal image can serve as a way to motivate, inspire, or empower change. For example,

> *Your ideal image is the ever-changing illusion of who you think you should be, what you think you should have, or what you think you should do.*

it seems reasonable that if you feel flawed, you'd be able to fix that feeling by attaining a better version of yourself. Or that if you believe you are lacking an important quality, improving yourself would make the awful feeling go away. It seems reasonable that if you feel not-enough because you are single and lonely, finding a loving relationship would fix the problem. It seems perfectly rational that if you feel not-enough and blame your thighs, thinner thighs would fix the problem. Or that more money would fix the problem of feeling like a financial loser. Or that more success would fix the problem of feeling like a failure. Or that sacrificing even more of yourself would make your loved ones happy.

The feeling of inadequacy is very painful, but there's been a terrible misunderstanding—one that has cost us countless dollars, buckets of tears, and years of our lives. For me, the misunderstanding sounded like this: If I could just make more money, find a guy who really loves me, have thinner thighs, and be a better mom, I'd finally feel like enough.

This misguided notion is why I kept hustling and striving toward the ideal image, hoping to fill the terrible sense of lack, to mend my inadequacies, in hopes that I'd someday land in a place of worthiness. But even if I had a good mom day, good hair day, or good thigh day, there would always be a new problem, a new thing to fix. The pain of not-enoughness never subsided because I had it completely backward. The painful lack and unworthiness wasn't caused by my inability to attain my ideal image; it was caused by my lack of awareness of true self. I spent decades of my life focused on my ideal thighs, my ideal successes, the ideal dude who might possibly love me. The more time, attention, and energy I gave to the ideal image of who I hoped to become, the less time, attention, and energy I gave to who I truly was at my core.

To build self-worth, you must do the opposite. You need to value the true self more than the ideal image. Rather than chasing your idealized fantasy, you must pour your time and effort into being a caretaker of the true essence of who *you* are.

To be clear, nothing is fundamentally wrong with having an ideal image. It's perfectly normal to want more romance, a better body, a bigger house, or thicker hair. Nothing's wrong with wanting to serve your family, your friends in the best way possible. Nothing's wrong with investing yourself in a vocation, in academic or creative pursuits. Yet when the ideal image is valued, regarded, and cared for more than who you truly are, that's when you run into problems. When your

> *Rather than chasing your idealized fantasy, you must pour your time and effort into being a caretaker of the true essence of who you are.*

awareness is chronically fixated on the *image of who you think you should be*, your true self atrophies and self-worth deteriorates. This diminished sense of self becomes a painful sense of lack, of not being enough, of not being whole, of being worth *less*. And this creates a vicious cycle.

THE WORTHLESS CYCLE

The worthless cycle is a circle composed of three points each leading to the next—the story, the behavior, and the resulting reinforcement of the story. At the core of the worthless cycle is your valuation of the ideal image over the true self.

The cycle starts with a worthless story. A worthless story is any story that exalts or glorifies the ideal image while ignoring or disrespecting the true self. This story can sound like *I hate my hair*—a criticism about not living up to the ideal image. It can also sound like *I wish my hair were thicker*—a fantasy about attaining the ideal image. It can sound abusive: *I'll never amount to anything*. And it can sound oddly

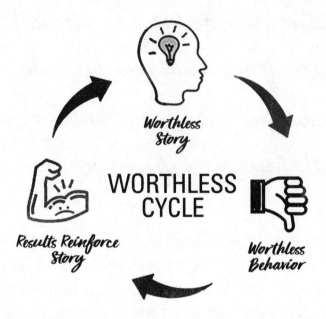

optimistic: *If I just keep trying, I'll eventually be perfect!* In the next chapter, we'll go into more detail about these stories, how to recognize them, and how to work with them. But for right now, just know that stories hold power and that you can usually spot a worthless story because even though the story might promise a worthy future, in the moment, it makes you feel worthless.

Whether you're the author of the worthless story in your head or merely repeating a worthless story that was once told to you, that story will affect your behavior. Whether you are conscious of them or not, your beliefs affect the way you act. This means that your stories influence your behavior and your reactions. Worthless behavior is any action or inaction that ignores, disrespects, or is indifferent to the true self.

Worthless behavior leads to worthless consequences. When your actions ignore the needs of your inner self, you end up devaluing your true self. Your true self becomes worth *less*.

From this worthless place, you fuel the original worthless story. This cycle repeats, spiraling downward into a special kind of hell, gaining momentum and power until there is no more *true self* value left.

To get out of the worthless cycle, it's easiest to start with something tangible and small. The goal here is to change your strategy to one that builds worthiness. Luckily, you don't have to tackle the largest problems of your life to start building worthiness. Rather than beginning with the most difficult or ingrained areas of your life—your marriage, your career, your body image—you can choose an easier subject. By focusing on small and unexpected corners of your life, it's much easier to flip the switch from worthlessness to worthiness.

> *By focusing on small and unexpected corners of your life, it's much easier to flip the switch from worthlessness to worthiness.*

THE WORTHY CYCLE

The worthy cycle works just like the worthless cycle but in the opposite direction. Rather than spiraling downward toward worthlessness, the worthy cycle is a circle composed of three points—the story, the behavior, and the resulting reinforcement of the story—that build self-worth. At the core of the worthy cycle is the valuing of your true self over the ideal image. It starts with a worthy story—any story that demonstrates that your true self is worth your own time, energy, and effort. You can find a worthy story by asking your true self: *What do you love? What do you desire? How would you be represented here?* If you're not clear on which category a story falls in (worthless or worthy), a quick way to check is to think of the true self like an innocent child and imagine telling a child the same message. If you would say it to an innocent child, it's probably a worthy story.

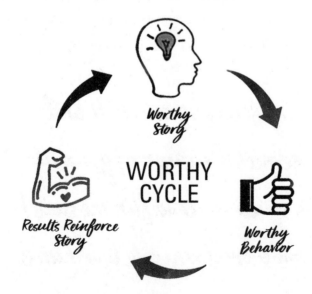

Worthy Story

WORTHY CYCLE

Results Reinforce Story

Worthy Behavior

Worthy behavior comes from worthy stories. Worthy behavior is any action or inaction that shows respect, care, and kind regard for your true self. This type of behavior leads to consequences that ultimately reinforce the worthy story.

The best way to move yourself into the worthy cycle is to take a deliberate action that reinforces the idea that *you*—not your ideal image—are worth time, attention, and energy. This is why I offer worthy work assignments to help open your eyes to unexpected areas of your life where you are in the worthy or worthless cycles rather than starting with a dramatic overhaul of the most challenging part of your life. For most of us, it's quite a bit easier to change a doormat, sweep the floor, or put laundry in the hamper than to quit a mind-numbing job or overhaul our entire financial plan. Yet surprisingly, small steps are just as effective as large ones at getting you into the worthy cycle.

> The best way to move yourself into the worthy cycle is to take a deliberate action that reinforces the idea that you—not your ideal image—are worth time, attention, and energy.

By taking small, worthy action steps, you immediately stop the downward spiral by placing intentional value on your true self. Any action that cares for your precious true self will help you accumulate more *self*. More *self* means more self-worth.

The worthy cycle builds on itself and gains upward momentum. Worthy behavior creates worthy consequences. Seeing the consequence of this new behavior (the new door-mat, the swept floor, the hamper) reinforces a worthy story, which inspires more worthy behavior, and so on.

WORTHY WORK: YOUR FRONT DOOR

Your first assignment is to take a picture of your front door. Don't move anything and don't change anything. Just take a picture of your door as is and study the photo.

Whether you live alone, in an apartment building, or out somewhere on a country road, you probably have a front door. (And if you don't, that's also quite telling.) This door is the boundary between your private world and your public world. It holds clues about who you are, how you live, and what you think you're worth. You walk in and out this door countless times a day. Every day for months. Years even.

And whether you know it or not, this door tells a story. But it's a story that's really easy to miss. It's a story that you might not see—even when you're looking straight at it. This is why I suggest taking a picture and studying the photo.

Because we all often become blind to what's in front of us for prolonged periods of time.

Selective attention is the ability to focus on particular objects or details instead of becoming overwhelmed by all the information available. If you're watching a basketball game, selective attention helps you focus on the ball rather than on every player and the referees and the cheering crowd in the background. But selective attention can also become a liability when you become so focused on one particular thing that you become unintentionally blind to critical objects and details.

We've all experienced the phenomenon of not seeing something that's right in front of us, whether it's the milk in the fridge, the reading glasses on the table, or the phone that you're already holding in your hand. Your ability to tune out what's unnecessary is often incredibly helpful, but it can become a liability when it comes to worthiness. Over time, you get used to what you focus on. You'll stop noticing where you're ignoring yourself. You won't see the gradual progression into worthlessness.

When I'm looking at someone's door photo, there's a certain mindset I hold, and I want you to hold this mindset when you look at the picture of your own front door, so let me explain. It's impossible for me to know what a student truly thinks, feels, or believes. Because behavior is often unconscious, it's also difficult for me (or my students) to know the truth about their habitual actions or inactions. However, if I take a close look at their photos, I can usually find evidential consequences of their behavior. To be specific, I look for anything that seems to be a reinforcement that they don't believe they are worth their own time, energy, or attention.

I want you to take a photo of your front door because a photo often disrupts the problem of selective attention. By studying the photo and zooming into details, you may see things that you've become habitually blind to. If you struggle with self-worth, by definition, you are lacking a valuable sense of *self*, so you'll need to rely on visible clues to show you the evidence of how you're reinforcing unconscious stories. I want you to look at your photos like a detective would look over a crime scene. In your case, the crime is against *you*, and you're looking for any clue that points to ignoring, disrespecting, or being indifferent to who you really are. That may sound a little funny when you're thinking about a front door. But I assure you, your front door holds a vault of information.

To give you an idea of how this works, let me share a few examples.

REAL STORIES: JENNIFER

When I first met Jennifer, she was decades into the worthless cycle. She said she signed up for my class because she felt like her marriage was failing and she desperately wanted to save it. She felt like her husband didn't love her.

"How long ago did you start feeling like this?" I asked.

"In the limo, on the way to our wedding," she said, half whispering. She was tender and ashamed as she told me about her wedding day and how she was worried that he wouldn't show up. Even then, she didn't feel worthy of his love, worthy of him, worthy of marriage. She'd felt like their relationship was an accident and that at any moment, he might wake up and change his mind. She knew he'd had affairs before and after their wedding, and she confided that she never quite felt like he'd chosen her. She said the most terrifying moment of her life was hearing the wedding march and thinking that she'd walk down the aisle to find no one standing there. My heart ached for her. By the time she signed up for my class, they'd been married for over twenty years. For twenty years, she had felt like a bride who could be left at any moment. For twenty years, she had continued to try to sell him on the reasons he should be with her, love her, commit to her.

While she focused on the illusion of who she thought she should be, the marriage that she hoped to have, and what she thought she needed to do to attain it, she lost focus and devalued her true self.

In the photo of Jennifer's front door, there was a large pile of muddy man-sized work boots to the right of the door. The doormat was utilitarian—dark brown and worn thin. The white wall near the door was stained and scuffed near the boot pile. A garden rake and a snow shovel leaned up against a metal sign. I zoomed in to read the sign—not her last name. Behind the glass weather door, I could see a dead Christmas wreath, even though the photo was taken in April. I saw nothing that reflected any hint of Jennifer living there. Not a shoe, not a detail, not even her name.

When she reflected on the photo, she said it was painfully obvious how much it represented the focus on her husband and the ideal image she wanted to create—a happy marriage— and how the only evidence that she even existed was the dead wreath, long forgotten—also symbolic. I asked her about the sign. She'd never even thought to question whether her name should also be on the sign on her own front door.

REAL STORIES: ASHLEY

Another woman, Ashley, signed up for my class to help her work through the guilt that she'd been carrying about her divorce. She'd left her husband three years prior and had since been paying the mortgage on their old house (where her ex now lived) as well as rent for her new home. She was cash-strapped and trying to make ends meet as a single mother of three. When I asked her why she'd taken full financial responsibility for their family, she said, "Because I left and ruined his life. I feel responsible for him. It's all my fault."

She couldn't even look at me and seemed to be burning with shame. I could tell how much she believed her story, how responsible she felt to her ex-husband and to the kids, and how desperate she was for any sense of relief from her guilt. She had spent three years trying to pay back an emotional debt with real dollars and she'd lost herself in the process. Her worthless story was not only that she ruined her ex's life but also their kids' lives. Her story didn't show any regard for her own self, the true self who had decided to leave the marriage, the true self who cared deeply for her kids, the true self who was desperately trying to create a better life; it offered no respect for her own wishes, her own pain, her own life. Rather, the story was focused on the illusory ideal of who she thought she should be, what she thought she should have done, and what she thought she should continue to do.

Ashley's front door was a nondescript wooden entrance to what looked like a run-down condo duplex. In the photo, I could see a kid's bike and helmet, a few backpacks, and two pairs of ice skates. A dirt-filled plastic plant container stood nearby, and a tattered Christmas-themed doormat with "Let It Snow" scripted across it lay on the ground. This photo was taken in July. When Ashley shared it with me, she said that the most striking thing she saw was that it didn't look as if a successful professional lived there. She said it was almost like she was trying to make herself look poorer than she actually was. The bikes and skates and even the doormat were all things chosen by her kids. Nothing in the picture represented her. Nothing showed the new life she was trying to create. If the door represented anything, it was the penance that she thought she owed.

REAL STORIES: PATRICIA

When Patricia signed up for class, she shared that she had an intense fear of other people not liking her. She hated conflict and did her best to always put others first—her kids, her friends, her work, her marriage. She was frustrated by her pattern, what she called "always playing small," but confided that the most painful area of her life was her body. She said that for as long as she could remember, she equated the size of her body with her self-worth.

She said, "It is so pervasive, I can't eat what I want unless the size of my body is 'right.' I can't enjoy a moment of vacation. I can't buy the clothes I want. I can't truly relax. What I eat and how I look are directly tied to my worth as a human being."

Patricia's worthless story was centered around the ideal image of the body she thought she should have, the size she thought she should be. This story is a recipe for disaster when it comes to self-worth. Rather than working to take up space and claim more self, Patricia's behavior was centered around erasing, shrinking, and controlling herself. And this never works because there's no way to become small enough—metaphorically or physically—to make you feel like you deserve to take up the space you need. The smaller she got, the less self she owned, creating a painful sense of lack that reinforced her idea that she needed to become even smaller. And the only end to this vicious circle would be to erase herself completely.

Patricia's photo showed a glossy, jet-black double door and a simple but elegant black doormat centered in front. The stoop was flanked by pristine white pillars. On either side of the doorway, there was a large, glossy black planter containing a perfectly manicured topiary and a glossy black Adirondack chair with a large black-and-white striped pillow that looked more for show than for sitting. There was not a leaf or pillow out of place, and not even a speck of dust was visible. When Patricia reflected on this photo, she confessed that even though everything in the photo looked perfect, there were flaws that you couldn't see. The doorway was the outward symbol of her ideal image—perfect, manicured, and flawless—and her story about it was that it still wasn't good enough. She said the back sides of the pillows were stained, the topiaries had spiderwebs in them, and there were fingerprints around the doorknob. I pushed her further, asking her to reflect through the eyes of her true self, asking her if this photo represented her inner Patricia, what she loved, and what she cared for.

Her voice cracked, and she took a long pause before speaking. "No," she said. "I hate black and white. It feels so sterile, so uptight. I don't like having to keep everything perfect. I'm so tired of trying to keep everything perfect."

Stopping the cycle—for Jennifer, Ashley, and Patricia—would require a complete change of strategy. I'd love to say that with a few magic words, Jennifer would feel loved and wanted, Ashley would stop feeling guilty, and Patricia would start taking up more space, but that's never the case. A feeling of worthlessness doesn't happen overnight. It happens over years and decades. And the longer one has been in the worthless cycle, the more power their stories hold, the more unconscious their behavior becomes, and the more evidence there is to fuel the stories.

To get out of the worthless cycle, the next phase of the front door assignment is to complete a simple front door makeover. The key concept here is to *do* something. This means that you intentionally change your behavior and take action in a way that reinforces that your true self is worth time, attention, and energy. This is how you change strategies and start building self-worth. By taking action that places value on your true self, you move yourself into the worthy cycle.

Your front door makeover will be a powerful reminder and anchor for this work. Rather than walking through a door that unintentionally reinforces worthlessness countless times a day, you'll walk through a doorway that reminds you of your own worthiness. This doesn't mean that you have to buy a bunch of stuff or that you have to remodel your home. It simply means that you put a little effort toward respecting and caring for your true self by changing your behavior and giving yourself evidence of a new story.

To do this, you'll have to check in with your true self and ask *What do you love? What do you desire? How would you be represented here?*

Jennifer went to work on her front door right away. She took down the wreath and threw away the ratty mat. She ordered a new sign for the door—one with her last name next to her husband's—and picked up a cute and colorful doormat. She sponged the dirt off the wall, put the boots in a basket, and moved the rake and snow shovel into the garage. These were small changes, but every time she came home, she noticed how different she felt. Where she'd previously fallen into the habit of focusing on an ideal image of her marriage, she now had a visible reminder of her own self, her own life, and her own wishes every time she walked through the front door. This tangible change helped her gain clarity about the greater changes that she would need to face in her life. By being reminded that she needed to show up as her true self, she paved a way to begin confronting the problems in her marriage.

Ashley's work was centered around allowing herself to own her new life. She began her front door makeover by investing in two beautiful pots, with brand-new plants, for either side of the threshold. She wanted these plants to be the outward symbol for the new life that she was trying to create. She didn't have much of a green thumb, so she simply committed to doing her best with the plants and replacing them if they stopped thriving. Where she used to come home to a pot of dirt and a pile of kids' toys, she was now greeted by two happy green plants. She was surprised by how much she loved those plants and how much care she wanted to give them. These outward symbols of her true self were a daily reminder to care for the life that she deserved to live.

Patricia's focus on her ideal image had kept her uptight and perfectionistic. She checked in with her inner self and asked, *What do you love? What do you desire? How would you be represented here?* Then she confessed with a giggle, "I think my true self just wants to relax." So we decided that her work would be around allowing herself some imperfection and ease. She remembered that during college, she used to love going to flea markets and thrift stores, so she took an afternoon off and found a few vintage markets and thrift stores to visit, to see if it felt like something that would honor her true self. She was amazed at the simple joy and silliness of it and was thrilled to find a funky orange chair that seemed to be the exact opposite of uptight and perfect. It wasn't beautiful or new, but it was fun and it made her smile, so she brought it home and replaced the glossy black Adirondack chair on her front porch. She brought out an old colorful patchwork quilt of her grandma's that she'd long ago stored away. She realized that her true self prioritized having things that she loved and couldn't care less about having a perfect black-and-white decor. Patricia's front door still had a classic and elegant look, but now it had a bit more color, imperfection, and character thrown in. Every time she came home, Patricia still felt the urge to make everything perfect and caught herself wanting to put the funky things away where no one would see them. I reminded her that this was her old worthless story rearing its head and to instead use the chair and quilt to reinforce her worthy story. Her front door became a reminder that her true self, regardless of how imperfect, also deserved her time, attention, and energy. This little bit of looseness at her doorstep started to permeate the rest of her life.

YOUR WORTHY WORK

Very important: Under no circumstances are you allowed to do this exercise with the intention of self-shaming, adding to your to-do list, or causing yourself overwhelming shame spirals or anxiety. This exercise is only to be done with compassion and love.

Now it's your turn. Take a picture of your front door. Don't move anything, and don't change anything.

Just take a picture of your door as it is in this moment, and study the photo. Look for clues or evidence that shows a disregard of true self. Check in with your true self and ask *What do you love? What do you desire? How would you be represented here?* Determine a few small changes that you can make to your front door to reinforce the idea that your true self is worth your time, attention, and energy. By taking action to respect and care for your true self, your front door will become a daily reinforcement of worthiness. Take an after picture, and journal about your findings.

JOURNALING PROMPTS

1. Find an example from your life where you fall into the worthless cycle. What story begins the cycle for you? How do you behave when you believe that story? How does your behavior reinforce the original story?

2. Find an example from your life where you can choose the worthy cycle. What story begins the cycle? How do you behave when you believe that worthy story? How does your behavior reinforce the original story?

3. Describe what you observed in your front door photo. What did you learn about yourself?

CHAPTER 2
Worthless and Worthy Stories

Sometimes you hear it before you even get out of bed in the morning. Sometimes it waits until you grab your phone and start scrolling through Instagram. Sometimes you hear it most when you're searching your closet for something to wear. Or maybe when you're leaning over your bathroom sink, putting on mascara. It infiltrates your day, no matter what you're doing or where you're going.

Regardless of the trigger, the voice is familiar. It's the voice telling you that you're not enough. Not strong enough, powerful enough, smart enough, pretty enough. It's the voice that tells you that you're not measuring up, keeping up, or speaking up.

Maybe the voice tells you that if you were just more disciplined, if you sacrificed more, served more, tried harder, if the stars were aligned just a little bit differently—maybe then you'd experience the elusive feeling of worthiness. Maybe then you'd feel like you matter, like you are good, wanted, loved. Maybe then you'd finally feel like you are enough. But no matter how hard you try, the voice always finds a gap between who you think you're supposed to be and who you actually are.

This is the voice that pipes up when you want to try something new, when you get ready for a date, when you think about applying for an exciting job, or when you dare to follow a dream. It's the voice that says you're ugly, old, or stupid. It's the voice that makes up stories about how you need to be better, faster, or more. This voice is a constant commentator about your life, a critic who follows you wherever you go. This voice ranks, judges, critiques, hassles, congratulates, and is all caught up in what other people are doing, what you look like, and what other people might be thinking of you.

This voice is obsessed with your *ideal image*. It has ideas about what your husband should or shouldn't be doing and what your son's coach should or shouldn't be doing. It talks about whether or not Sheila in accounting smiled at you in the right way. It has a laundry list of changes that it's constantly wanting to enforce. This voice is exhausting.

I call it a voice, but it often feels more solid, more permanent than an internal dialogue—more like just a fact of life, the way things are. It can feel more like a sixty-pound bag of shame, fear, and not-enough-ness that you tote around on your back all day. The feeling of not-enough-ness is at the heart of the worthless cycle, and it's not caused by your faults, your inadequacies, or by an objective lack of anything in your life. This feeling is kicked off by a story, a sentence, or a belief that is most often untrue. This feeling is caused by listening to the voice in your head, the aspect of your mind that's concerned with your ideal image. To end this cycle and start building self-worth, you'll need to not only recognize the worthless story that plays in your head, you'll also need to learn to recognize, understand, and work with the voice that authors your worthless stories.

> *The feeling of not-enough-ness is at the heart of the worthless cycle.*

THE VOICE IN YOUR HEAD

When I speak about the voice in your head, I am referring to the intangible world of your mind—thoughts, ideas, perceptions, beliefs, and imagination. The worthless voice narrates and repeats your worthless stories. It is the voice inside your head that's often critical, judgmental, envious, full of rage, or ready to bolt. This worthless voice can mimic voices from your past; it might do a brilliant impression of your mother, your second-grade teacher, or your ex-husband. It can grab pieces of past conversations—usually the things you wish you could forget—and embed them in your head like a Katy Perry song, replaying them over and over.

Even though this voice might sound like your own voice, the important thing to remember is that the voice isn't *you*. This voice is merely an aspect of your mind that functions like a software system running strategies to control and predict possible threats. The voice isn't personal. The voice isn't against you, trying to hurt your feelings, or trying to sabotage you. It is merely an aspect of your mind trying to make the world around you behave, to make it predictable so that you can be safe.

To be fair, this voice is only one aspect of your vast, complex, and beautiful mind. This voice comes from a tiny part of the brain called the amygdala. If you imagine drawing a line in between both of your ears and visualize two almonds positioned along that line, one behind each eye, you'd have a good idea of the general shape, size, location, and origin of this little beast of a voice. The almonds—amygdalae—are part of your limbic system. The limbic system, also known as the reptilian brain or the emotional brain, takes in information through your senses and attaches emotions to it.

The amygdala serves as the triage master for all incoming information. Information comes in through the senses, and those little almonds go to work sorting and ranking the potential threats, determining whether you're safe or at risk. When things are familiar and predictable, your little almonds are nice and quiet. But life on planet Earth is never all that predictable; reality is a constant barrage of things that change, things that are unfamiliar, and things that put us at risk, whether physically or emotionally. These perceived threats trigger the amygdala's fear/rage response, raising your brain's level of anxiety so you can pay attention and eliminate the threat.

When you understand the nature of this voice and its intentions, you'll see that it evolved for very important reasons. The voice is very helpful when you encounter something dangerous like a car skidding to a stop in front of you on the highway, a grease fire in your kitchen, or a black widow under the bathroom sink. The problem is that this voice in your head yells loudly no matter what the threat is: whether the house is on fire or your jeans aren't fitting right. To the mind voice, both are dangerous. Both are triaged as threats. To this aspect of your mind, everything is an emergency, and everything (and everyone) needs to be controlled. This primitive part of your brain was handed down from your ancestors, and it evolved to keep you fed, watered, warm, and safe from predators. It also kept you safe from acts of nature or attacks from neighboring tribes. It kept you safe within your own tribe so you weren't exiled, because that would have meant certain death.

Imagine all that history and all that beautiful programming that once kept humans safe from famine, flood, blizzards, and bear attacks, now being funneled into whether or not an Instagram post got enough likes, whether your coworker is talking behind your back, or whether someone swiped right.

Impending danger triggers a very old part of our brain, and when that part gets freaked out, the voice in your head can be a bit like an annoying car alarm going off at two in the morning—*eeee-ahhhh eeee-ahhhh woop woop woop*. It's difficult to have a clear thought, and it's nearly impossible to not react to the sound.

The good news is that, just like a car alarm, this voice evolved to keep you alert and safe, and it does a very good job at that when the threat is real. The bad news is, just like a car alarm, most of the time, there is no real threat, and until you shut it down, it'll keep blaring for no good reason. The work here is to train yourself not to react to the voice in your head and to see it more like that annoying car alarm in the middle of the night. It's to treat that voice more like background noise and less like an oracle for whether or not you measure up.

YOUR WORTHLESS STORY INFLUENCES YOUR BEHAVIOR

Whether you're conscious of it or not, the voice in your head affects what you do, when you do it, and how you do it. When you're working toward building your self-worth, it becomes imperative to notice your habitual stories and to become conscious of how your behavior reacts to these stories.

Whether you're conscious of it or not, the voice in your head affects what you do, when you do it, and how you do it.

Your mind automatically finds supporting evidence to reinforce its beliefs. It's like an algorithm that's on the hunt for fake news. When you believe a story like "You'll never succeed," your mind gets busy offering you supporting evidence. It filters through information to offer more and more proof to support the belief. It will remind you of that time that you were stupid enough to put yourself out there for class president, only to lose the election. It'll remind you of that bad blind date you went on last October. It'll replay that time when your best friend didn't come to your birthday party. It'll pull up current evidence, reminding you of those extra ten pounds you're carrying, or how you can never get your hair to look quite right, or how you always seem to be running five minutes late. It'll create evidence out of nothing; things that are purely coincidental will start being slanted toward proving the worthless story. Your neighbor didn't wave when you drove by, or you forgot to pick up milk at the store, or your friend didn't respond to a text. The mind starts to say, "See? I told you that you're worthless."

When you believe worthless stories about yourself, you behave differently from someone who doesn't believe the negative stories swirling around in their head. If you're walking around thinking that you're defective, you're going to behave in ways that then help your mind say, "See? I told you that you're defective." Worthless stories become self-fulfilling prophecies of worthlessness.

Sometimes it's hard to draw a clear line between these thoughts and the resulting behavior, so let's look at how this could play out in real life.

> *When you believe worthless stories about yourself, you behave differently from someone who doesn't believe the negative stories swirling around in their head.*

Imagine a woman who believes she is damaged, defective, and unwanted. Take a second to let her story sink in. Imagine really believing that you're damaged, defective, and unwanted. Think about how that story affects your physiology, your emotions, your sense of optimism. Now, let's imagine that the woman with the worthless story gets asked out on a date, and let's see how much power this story can have over the span of one simple night.

Worthless stories create worthless behavior, and this shows up quickly on a date. Her worthless story—*I'm damaged, defective, and unwanted*—will color every aspect of her behavior before, during, and after the date. It influences what she wears (loose clothes because she's ashamed of her figure), how she does her hair (she parts it so she covers an old scar on her forehead), and the shoes she chooses to put on her feet (she wants to appear small and demure, so she wears flats). It impacts how she responds to the date request (she canceled a movie night with her best friend because she didn't want to make the guy wait), how she walks into the restaurant (hands clasped in front of her, head down, shoulders rolled forward), how she smiles (quickly, without showing her teeth because she's self-conscious about her overbite), and whether she gives eye contact (only briefly). This belief winds itself around every word that she says or doesn't say. She's careful not to talk about anything too vulnerable and tries to keep the conversation focused on him. It affects the way she sits (her purse on her lap, hunched forward, arms crossed in front of her on the table), her posture (she keeps herself small by rounding her back and curving over the table), and her ability to follow the conversation. She's constantly thinking about her own inadequacies. (*Is my scar showing? Do I have something in my teeth? I hope he doesn't ask me about my job. Suck your stomach in... Wait, what were you saying?*) It affects her capacity to laugh; she's so caught up in her own damaged and unwanted self, she misses his smile, his jokes, his lightness. She's a hunched-over, deer-in-the-headlights, super self-conscious, tight little ball of a woman who seems a little damaged and defective and renders herself unwanted. By the end of the night, she has even more evidence to support the original story. By believing her mind's story that she's damaged, defective, and unwanted, she can't help but act damaged, defective, and unwanted, which gives her mind even more fuel to keep her stuck in the worthless cycle.

This is the part where my students usually ask, "But what if I *am* defective? What if I really do have something wrong with me? What if I really am unlovable? It feels so true!"

Well, of course it feels true. Your mind has been spewing this nonsense and working hard to gather evidence for a very long time. All your worthless stories are going to feel very true. But that doesn't make them true. It just means that they are heavily practiced.

The truth is more complicated than the voice in your head. The truth is that you are defective and so am I. And so is the dude across the table from you on that date. You are damaged and so am I. And so is that glamorous person up there on their pedestal. You are unwanted and you are wanted. You are unloved and you are loved. This isn't about getting to a place where you're just blowing smoke up your own ass. I'm not suggesting that you walk around telling yourself that you're perfectly awesome all the time. First, because it's not true; we are all flawed. And second, because it doesn't help in the realm of self-worth.

You gain self-worth by claiming more of your true self, not by thinking that you're awesome. Self-worth is not grandiosity. Grandiosity values the ideal image. Self-worth values the true self. When you value the true self, you allow the damage, you allow the defects, you allow the loved and the unloved parts of you. You hold them, you care for them, you own them.

Now let's imagine this woman gets asked out on a date, but this time, she has a very different story, one where she's not judging herself against her ideal image. One where she deeply wants and cares for her true self. She values who she is and is looking for someone who will also value who she is. This belief changes every aspect of her behavior before, during, and after the date.

It influences what she wears (she wears her favorite outfit with bright colors and chunky jewelry), how she does her hair (she pulls it back because she doesn't want to fuss with it), and the shoes she chooses to put on her feet (she loves the way her legs look in heels, so she wears her favorite pair of slingbacks). It impacts how she responds to the date request (rather than changing her plans, she was open and direct about her availability and found a time that worked for both of them), how she walks into the restaurant (chin up, shoulders back), how she smiles (big, showing her overbite and her endearing dimples), and whether she gives eye contact (she's not looking for his approval; she's checking in with herself to see how she feels about him, so yes, there's eye contact; she's curious about him and wants to know if they are a good fit). This belief winds itself around every word that she says or doesn't say. The conversation goes back and forth; she asks questions and he answers and vice versa. It affects the way she sits (shoulders back, leaning forward, hands animated), her posture (chin up, open heart, strong backbone), and her ability to follow the conversation. Her mind isn't cluttered with self-conscious thoughts; instead, she's focused on getting to know him and on showing up fully as herself. It affects her capacity to laugh; he's subtle and witty, and it catches her off guard. She breaks into a riot of laughter, head back and unbridled. She's a strong, self-possessed, relaxed, and open woman who seems like she values who she is and is looking for someone who will also value who she is because she is that woman.

This woman is listening to a different voice, a worthy voice, and her behavior and experience are radically different.

THE VOICE OF YOUR SOUL

The worthy voice is often subtle, even wordless. This voice is quieter, because it doesn't originate in the amygdala, nor is it programmed to protect you from threats. Rather, it comes from the intangible essence of your being. In some traditions, this part of you is called *spirit*; I happen to call it *soul*. Regardless of what you call it, it's the part of you that knows what wants to be lived through you. It's the part of you that has access to your inborn potential, something that psychologist James Hillman calls the acorn theory—the idea that your full potential is already encoded within you, just as the full potential of a mighty oak tree is encoded within a tiny acorn. The worthy voice speaks from the part of you that sees this encoded potential and helps navigate you toward it.

The soul has access to a more expansive perspective. It isn't bound by the confines of time, space, or rationality. It is able to connect to a greater, universal, or divine intelligence. It is deeply connected to your self-worth because it knows who you are beyond your ego, your programmed beliefs, your mind, your emotions, or even your body. It knows that you are worth your own time, energy, and effort.

Where the voice in your head is concerned with making life predictable and secure, the worthy voice has something else to protect. The worthy voice is in charge of protecting your true self, that vital source of you-ness that burns within you. The part of you that lights the fire of inspiration, the part of you that wants to grow into your own version of the majestic oak tree. The worthy voice is in charge of protecting what the true self loves and desires, what the true self wants to create, and how the true self wants to grow, expand, become, and evolve.

> *The worthy voice is in charge of protecting your true self, that vital source of you-ness that burns within you.*

LISTENING TO YOUR WORTHY VOICE

The worthy voice can be very subtle and easily missed. Even though it's often difficult to find your own worthy voice, I've found that you can almost always imagine what a caring teacher, your best friend, or your partner might say to lift you up in a given situation. By imagining the voices of people who truly love and respect you, you start to tune in to the frequency of the worthy voice, making it easier to hear your own.

One of the best tools for this is to create an imaginary committee of worthy voices. Imagine inviting five people to join you in a boardroom, at a round table, or at a small dinner party. You do not need to know these people personally, nor do they need to be alive. Even though this is an imaginary round table, it's a powerful exercise to help you access a worthy voice. Maybe you invite your grandmother, Oprah, your high school English teacher, Beyoncé, and Jesus. Regardless of whether your round table members are people you know intimately or people who may have passed long ago, you'll construct an inner committee that you can turn to in times when you might struggle to hear your own worthy voice. The point of this round table is to be able to imagine looking at yourself through the lens of worthiness. The only rule is that each member of the committee must see you as truly worthy and offer you a worthy perspective. To make lasting change, you must not only learn how to behave differently, you must learn how to tune in to an inner voice that will lead the way.

WORTHY STORIES CHANGE YOUR BEHAVIOR

By tuning in to the voice that protects your true self, your behavior will change significantly. Instead of behaving in ways that are focused on the ideal image, you take action from a place of honoring and respecting your true self. This means that the axis of your experience starts with you. From that center, you move your awareness outward toward those around you. You check in with who you are, how you feel, and what you want before moving your awareness to anyone or anything outside your true self.

This sounds simple, but trust me...it will take some practice. You're here with me because you're wanting to gain self-worth. That means that you've probably spent a good portion of your life listening to the voice in your head, landing you smack-dab in the worthless cycle. To override the voice in your head and supersede the influence of those little almonds in your brain, you're going to be up against a few hundred thousand years of evolution. This will take time and practice, but little by little, you'll learn to listen to the voice in your head just a bit less, and you'll learn to listen to the voice of your true self just a bit more. By taking small steps, you can learn how to shift your awareness away from that feel-bad voice and start to tune in to the subtler voice that will help to move you into the worthy cycle.

> *Little by little, you'll learn to listen to the voice in your head just a bit less, and you'll learn to listen to the voice of your true self just a bit more.*

Worthy work requires strong boundaries, and the first boundary you'll need to commit to is with the voice in your head. Imagine witnessing someone berating a child. Imagine someone talking to a sweet little baby in the way that the voice in your head talks to you. How long would it take for you to intervene? What emotion would come up?

When you witness abuse or malevolence against a vulnerable child, it's natural to want to protect them. It's appropriate to feel anger and to do what you can to remove the child from harm. This is the same attitude I want you to take with your true self.

To be clear, that voice in your head isn't *trying* to be harmful; it's merely doing what it evolved to do. Yet when left unchecked, that voice can do a lot of damage. When your intention is to care for your true self, you'll need to do what you can to interrupt the voice in your head and immediately honor and respect your true self.

Any time you notice a worthless voice commenting on a part of your life, I want you to stop what you're doing and depersonalize the voice. Remember that the voice is like the car alarm going off at two in the morning. It's annoying, but you don't have to react to it. Consciously pull your awareness away from the worthless message, and focus on your true self. You can use the image of your true self, or you can use the image of a young child if that helps you. By bringing your attention away from the worthless voice and focusing on your true self, you'll interrupt the pattern and create some space for the quieter worthy voice to be heard.

> By bringing your attention away from the worthless voice and focusing on your true self, you'll interrupt the pattern and create some space for the quieter worthy voice to be heard.

For example, imagine that you're getting ready for a vacation and you need a new swimsuit. Which means... you guessed it...swimsuit shopping. Maybe I'm stating the obvious, but this is the type of situation where the worthless voice can get really loud, really fast. Even as I sit here writing this, I can hear the voice in my head saying, "Oh, hell no. You do *not* need a swimsuit. No one wants to look at that." Within the span of a few seconds, I've forgotten my true self and I'm measuring myself against an ideal image. I can feel the power of this voice; even though I'm simply writing a fictional example, I already feel the effects of the voice: shame, fear, disgust, and panic. I immediately feel like I want to retreat and give up.

This is where I have to stop myself. Take a breath and interfere. Even if I think that voice is correct. Even if I agree with everything the voice is saying. Especially if I agree with the voice, I must interrupt the pattern and redirect my attention.

This doesn't mean that I slingshot myself over to "I have the best body in the world! Who wouldn't want to check this out? Let me at those bikinis..."

No. That's not a realistic attitude, nor is it helpful.

The worthy voice isn't going to be the polar opposite of the worthless voice. It's going to be simpler, kinder, and focused on your true self rather than the ideal image. To find this voice, I close my eyes and imagine speaking to my true self. What does she want? What would honor and respect this innermost essence of who I am?

What I find is that deep inside me, there's a person who just wants permission to play in the water. She wants the freedom to swim. She wants to cool off when it's hot. This has nothing to do with whether or not I have stretch marks or cellulite. This is an interior voice that wants to live the fullest experience that life offers. This is an interior voice that knows she deserves to swim comfortably regardless of how her body measures up to her ideal image.

This is where instead of listening to the voice in my head, I choose to honor my true self. I imagine speaking to the small child within me who's hoping for permission, and I offer myself the permission. I might even say the words out loud, "You're allowed to play in the water. You're allowed to have fun."

By interrupting the worthless voice and tuning in to the worthy voice, I have a completely different experience. Instead of being focused on what my body looks like or what other people might think, I focus on what the water will feel like or what might be comfortable against my skin.

HOW TO CHANGE THE STORY FROM WORTHLESS TO WORTHY

In the pursuit of building self-worth, disengaging from the worthless voice is crucial. The practice is to set a boundary with this voice. This means that as soon as you become conscious of any worthless story, you'll interrupt the pattern, redirect, and refocus. Over time, you'll stop taking that voice so seriously, and you'll begin to see it more like you would a faulty car alarm. Instead of allowing it to consume your attention, you'll get better at minimizing your emotional reaction, redirecting your attention, and consciously focusing on a worthy story.

If the goal is to stop taking it all so seriously, how do you do that? How exactly do you stop reacting to a message that makes you feel so terrible?

One of my favorite quotes on writing is from Hemingway's memoir, *A Moveable Feast.* In the book, he mentions what he'd say to himself if he found himself stuck, unable to get a story going. He offered, "All you have to do is write one true sentence. Write the truest sentence that you know."

This advice is profound, not only for writers but also for someone who wants to build a stronger sense of self-worth. If you typed up all your worthless thoughts in a twenty-four-hour period, you'd have a lot of random nonsense, a lot of fear and worry and judgment. Sorting through thousands of thoughts and grievances and worries, is there even one thought that you'd keep as undeniably true? My guess is no.

LEAN INTO THE TRUTH

Truth is a sweet spot for the mind, an axis, a point of stabilization. It gives your mind focus, creating a sense of calm, harmony, and safety. It gives the mind something to hold on to, something to trust. One true sentence has the power to calm the mind. Focusing on one true thing, you find stillness. To quickly reduce the power of the worthless voice and to redirect your attention to the worthy voice, ask yourself to state one true thing, the truest thing you know.

In my swimsuit shopping example, one true thing may have been *I love to swim.* Or one other true thing may have been *I want permission to have fun.* Or another true thing may have been *It's okay that this is difficult.*

The one true thing doesn't necessarily have to be a super perky life-coach-y thought. To interrupt the pattern, you only have to say something true.

> *You are not the voice in your head;*
> *you're the one listening to it.*

For example, one true thing may be *I am deeply identified with what my body looks like.* This isn't a great story, but it is surprisingly relieving to admit this to myself. One true thing gets you out of that ideal image–obsessed voice and redirects toward a more intimate relationship of self. The truth offers solid ground to stand on. One true thing, even when the truth isn't pretty, helps alleviate the sense of not-enough-ness. By giving your mind a point of focus, you remember that you are not the voice in your head; you're the one listening to it.

Now you try.

1. Think of a situation where you often feel not enough, ashamed, or unworthy.
2. Imagine the story that plays in your head during this situation. What worthless message does your mind offer up?
3. Now set a boundary with that story. Instead of believing the story or allowing it to influence your emotions or behavior, take a moment to intentionally put that message

in "faulty car alarm" category. Even though the message might be difficult to ignore, see if you can remove your internal reaction from the mental noise.

4. Redirect by asking yourself: What is one true thing? What is the truest thing I know? Tap into a deeper and wiser part of your consciousness by bringing your attention to the truth.

5. Journal your findings.

WORTHY WORK: YOUR TRUE SELFIE

Before you read further, let's get started with your next assignment. I want you to take a full-length picture of yourself as is right now. Don't change your clothes. Don't wait for the day that you look cute. (Seriously, I want you to take the picture of exactly what you look like on a typical day. Your Instagram-worthy selfie self isn't your true self and can't help you build self-worth.) Just take a picture of yourself as you are in this moment, and study the photo.

Just like with the front door exercise, I recommend using a photograph because we tend to become blind to the little details in our lives, and a photo can help us take an inventory that's more accurate.

When I'm looking at my students' full-length selfie pictures, I'm first checking for whether or not they look comfortable in the picture. I'm not necessarily looking at what they are wearing, how they have their hair done, or whether they are smiling. Worthiness is built by prioritizing the true self. Sometimes that looks like a woman in a messy bun, bare feet, and yoga pants. Sometimes it looks like a man in a thousand-dollar suit. Sometimes it looks like a mother wearing pajamas printed with pink penguins, and sometimes it looks like a woman in a pencil skirt and slingback heels. My detective eye is searching for whether this person is reinforcing the idea that their true self is worth their time, attention, and energy or if they're ignoring their true self and working to promote their ideal image. Basically, I'm looking for clues about whether this person is reinforcing the worthy cycle or reinforcing the worthless cycle through the way they dress or their grooming and beauty practices. I'm looking for evidence that points to whether they believe they deserve their own respect and attention.

To give you an idea of how this works, let me share a few examples.

REAL STORIES: MARY

Mary, a yoga teacher and wellness consultant, had recently received her degree in acupuncture and had just opened her own wellness studio. She worried about the success of her business in her small, conservative mountain town. She signed up for the Worthy Project to overcome her insecurities around marketing her new business. When I looked at Mary's selfie, I immediately noticed a plastic quality in her smile. Her body looked rigid and overly posed with her hand on her hip, her head tipped to the side, and her chin slightly raised. It almost gave off the air of confidence, but more so she appeared like someone who was comfortable playing a role for the camera. The persona in the photograph was quite different from the person I had seen in class. Typically, she was genuine, forthright, and inquisitive. Her physical appearance usually had a balance of grace and comfort. Her clothes were typically cozy, her hair often pushed back off her face.

Yet here in the picture, she looked like she'd been styled from head to toe. Her hair was pulled to the side and curls cascaded over one shoulder. Her clothes, although beautiful, looked rigid and pinched. Her white shirt was neatly tucked into a tight pair of light-washed jeans. Her petite frame was overwhelmed by tall boots, riding up past her knees. I saw nothing that resembled the woman I'd come to know in class.

When she shared the stories that came up when she looked at her photo, they seemed to all focus on what she was wearing. She spoke about her boots, her earrings, her hair, the jeans. Her answers were focused primarily on the outfit, the look, the adornments—on the ideal image she'd hoped to portray.

When I asked if there was any evidence in the picture that seemed to reinforce the worthless cycle, she said, "The first thing I notice is my posture. I seem guarded and uptight. It's almost like the real me has disappeared behind the woman in the picture. I also notice that I don't really love these boots. I bought them to impress a guy, and now I keep wearing them trying to prove to myself that it was money well spent. When I look at this picture, I don't see a lot of true self. I see a lot of thought put into impressing others."

Her worthless story, "I need to impress others," led to worthless behavior of purchasing boots that she didn't even like. By wearing the boots, she reinforced worthlessness and continued the cycle.

The next step was to change the story in her head to align with her true self. Her new worthy story became "I need to honor my true self." Rather than trying to impress anyone else or trying to prove that money was well spent, she chose to honor herself.

When she shared the one small change she could make, she said, "I no longer feel compelled to keep wearing the boots. I don't have to prove to myself that they were worth the money. They served their purpose, and I learned my lesson. I think I'm going to donate the boots and go get the pair of clogs that I've been wanting."

When she posted her after picture, she looked more like the relaxed and self-possessed woman I'd known her to be in class. She still had on the white T-shirt and blue jeans, but she now looked more comfortable and less like she was trying to impress. Her hair cascaded over her shoulders as she leaned into the camera with a big smile, both hands pointing to her outstretched leg, highlighting her new gray clogs. She said, "I can't tell you how much these shoes make me smile. They are like a little celebration on my feet. I just love them."

Her new story, "I need to honor my true self," led to worthy behavior of purchasing shoes that celebrated her true self. By wearing the shoes, she reinforced worthiness, strengthening her sense of self-worth.

REAL STORIES: KATRINA

Katrina, an office manager and mother of two adult children, signed up for my class to help her feel a sense of purpose in this new and unfamiliar era of midlife. She'd had a strong sense of who she was when the kids were home. She said, "I was busy raising kids, going to work, helping out at school. I didn't have time to even think about my self-worth. Now that they're grown and gone, I thought I'd be ready for some self-care, but I don't even know where to start. I feel lost and unsure of myself." When I looked at Katrina's picture, I first noticed her smile. In the photo, her phone was in front of her face, but her wide smile couldn't be contained or obscured. She seemed bright and lively. She didn't seem like she was taking herself too seriously, and her levity and her willingness to do the work shone through. She wore a baggy black shirt with a long black sweater over it, shapeless black pants, and clunky black shoes. Her dark, formless clothes were a stark contrast to her bright, smiling face.

She shared that her worthless story was "I'm too fat," which was the typical voice she listened to when she got dressed in the morning. She had been told that black would help conceal her flaws. She was ashamed of her body and didn't want anything formfitting. Hence the black, oversize clothes.

When she looked at the photo through her detective eyes, she said that wearing plain-Jane clothes and too much black reinforced worthlessness for her. She said, "My personality is vibrant. I love color. I love to laugh, and I'm a little on the wild side. Dressing in utilitarian clothes is the opposite of what my true self wants."

Katrina decided that one small change would be to always add a pop of color. "For the first time in a long time, I'm actually excited to go shopping. Instead of thinking about covering up my body, I get to focus on finding something bright and beautiful." She cut ideas out of magazines and created a collage for inspiration: an aquamarine handbag, a lime-and-tangerine scarf, leopard-print ballet flats, a hot-pink sweater. Even though she didn't have the budget to go buy a new wardrobe, she took action that reinforced her sense of self-worth. Every time she found something bright and colorful, she'd pin it to her collage, an outward reminder to honor her true self.

REAL STORIES: LAUREN

Lauren signed up for my class in hope of gaining confidence as a new mom. She'd left a successful career as a website designer, and now, as a stay-at-home mom, she was struggling to define her new role and the expectations that went with it. Motherhood was messier and more chaotic than she'd thought it would be. She said, "I'm usually good at things, but this is so hard. I'm afraid that something is fundamentally wrong with me. How can so many women make this look so easy?" In Lauren's picture, she was barely visible. There were toys everywhere, laundry folded in stacks on the couch, and piles of paperwork smeared across the coffee table. Beyond the clutter, I saw a young mother doing her best to smile for the camera with a toddler on her hip. It looked like she was wearing her husband's T-shirt and sweatpants; both looked worn out and too large for her small frame. My heart went out to her; early motherhood is a difficult time in so many ways, and it's easy to lose focus on your true self and begin to compare yourself to an ideal image.

When I asked her what she saw in this picture, Lauren said, "A woman completely failing at motherhood." She mentioned the laundry that wasn't done, the toys that overcrowded her living room, and the stack of work that she never seemed to have time for. She said everything in the picture just reinforced worthlessness. "All I can see is how I'm not a good enough mom. Everything is a mess. I don't finish my work. I can't even get dressed. It's like everywhere I look, I'm reminded of how I'm not enough."

When she checked in with her true self, she found an inner desire for her own space. She had been trying to multitask motherhood, household chores, and work from her living room. She said, "I need to do something that just feels like me. I need a space that feels like mine. I need to wear clothes for me, not for the baby. I need to stop mixing everything together."

The first thing Lauren did was to get clear on how she wanted to use the spaces in her home. Rather than try to play with a toddler, work, and do laundry from the same space, she took the toys into the baby's room, moved her work to her office, and put the laundry on top of the washer and dryer. By making this small change, she was able to honor her need for space and for organization. When she was in mom mode, she played on the floor and engaged fully. When she needed to work, she went to the office. When she did laundry, she didn't let it consume the rest of her life. Instead of being focused on whether she measured up to the ideal image of motherhood, Lauren now had a little bit of open space to simply be herself.

YOUR WORTHY WORK

Very important: Under no circumstances are you allowed to do this exercise with the intention of self-shaming, adding to your to-do list, or causing yourself overwhelming shame spirals or anxiety. This exercise is only to be done with compassion and love.

Now it's your turn. Take a look at your selfie. What small change can you make to help reinforce a sense of worthiness? This means that you deliberately do something that reinforces that you are worth your own time, attention, and energy. Mary, Katrina, and Lauren did this by taking a simple action step that reinforced worthiness. Mary went out and bought a pair of clogs. Katrina made an inspired collage of colorful ideas. Lauren created visual boundaries within her home so that she had some breathing room.

Look at your full-length selfie picture with your detective eye. What do you notice? Let's walk through the worthless cycle to see how the stories in your head and the evidence in the photo reinforce each other.

1. Story: Observe the worthless voice. What stories do you hear when you look at the photo? Jot those down, and try to record at least one sentence of that car-alarm voice blaring at you.

2. Behavior: Objectively look at the photo, and search for evidence of behaviors that confirm the worthless story. You're looking for clues of where there's a disregard for your true self. You're also looking for clues of where you glorify the importance of the ideal image.

3. Reinforcement: How does the evidence you see reinforce the worthless story in your head?

The next step is to stop the worthless cycle and begin the worthy cycle. Change the story in your head to align with your true self. Determine one small change to the way you dress or to your grooming and beauty practices that will reinforce the idea that your true self is valuable. Then do it—today. Do something that reminds you that you deserve your own respect and attention. The next time you look in the mirror, that small change will reinforce your new story, making the voice of your true self a tiny bit stronger.

JOURNALING PROMPTS

1. What are your earliest memories of worthless stories?
2. How old were you when you began believing them?

3. How have these early stories affected your life?

4. If you could go back and speak to your younger self, what worthy message would you offer her?

5. How would your life be different if you started to believe this worthy story from now on?

CHAPTER 3
Giving and Spending

Once upon a time, I spent a few thousand dollars on a Gucci dress. I was thirty-five years old, recently divorced, and brand new at being a single mom. My business was tanking, and I had no idea where my next paycheck was coming from. Dressed up, at that time in my life, meant wearing fancy jeans with a newer pair of flip-flops. I worked from home, mostly in my pajamas or yoga clothes. My credit cards were almost maxed, and I was reeling from white-hot rejection after my first few attempts at dating post-divorce. I was a walking raw wound, scared and desperate. Never in my life had I felt so broken, so alone, so unwanted.

Let's just say buying a Gucci dress shouldn't have been at the top of my list that day.

Shelter? Sure.

Sustenance? Yes.

Fashion? Not so much.

But this Gucci dress debacle demonstrates not only the power of a worthless story and the compelling influence of an ideal image, it also demonstrates how giving and spending play out in the realm of worthiness.

I don't know what possessed me to even dare to shift my eyes in the direction of a Gucci store on that particular day. I was visiting girlfriends out of town, and on a whim, we decided to go shopping. My version of shopping tended toward consignment stores and cheap clothing outlets. Their version of shopping looked more like Tiffany & Co., Prada, and Burberry, which is how I found myself standing in the middle of a very posh mall, gaping at a dress that took my breath away. It was a beautiful shade of turquoise, a delicate knit silk, designed on the bias, a hug-every-curve piece of art. It was elegant and rich. Spotlights were perfectly poised over the mannequin, and the exquisite dress fell gracefully over her plastic figure.

In that moment, I don't think I even really saw the dress. Instead, I saw a better version of me. I saw myself with money. I saw myself being adored by a man who loved me. I saw myself being a successful coach. I saw a taller, thinner, and prettier version of myself. I saw a me who was at ease, sophisticated, elegant, and wealthy. I saw a flawless mother who wore heels and Gucci dresses while cooking dinner and helping her daughter with homework. I saw the better me who had taken a different path, the me who had gone to an Ivy League college and married a rich guy. The me who had a big-ass diamond ring on her finger and drove my 2.5 kids to private school in my BMW.

To be clear, this wasn't just a dress—it was my gateway to worthiness, a golden ticket to who I thought I should be. It's as if my ideal image had come to life right in front of my eyes. And that devil in a blue dress was wearing Gucci.

Before I could blink, I was inside the store trying on the dress. As soon as I slipped it over my shoulders, I could tell there was a problem with the fit—a detail that I immediately set out to ignore. The dress hugged my curves and swayed and flowed when I walked. It was almost perfect, except for one tiny flaw—it pulled tight across my chest, and the plunging neckline stretched wide open. Like bare chest wide open. Like naked. The dress was unwearable as it was.

I wish I could tell you that standing there in front of the mirror, boobs out, was the moment when I woke up. I wish I could tell you that this was the moment when I realized that I was chasing a fantasy and had completely lost touch with who I truly was. Unfortunately, that's not what happened. Instead of snapping out of my ideal-image fog, I doubled down on the dream. I felt like I was too close to this thing that I wanted so desperately. And I couldn't give up. I refused to go home that night feeling like a broken reject once again.

So I immediately came up with a plan to buy something to wear under the dress, something lacy that might look like it was always supposed to be part of the outfit. The fact that the dress didn't fit right wasn't going to stop me. The fact that I was staring down half a million dollars in debt at the time didn't matter. Nor did the fact that the dress cost the equivalent of a few months' rent. None of these details were powerful enough to dissuade me from my mission. This wasn't about buying a dress; it was about trying to spend my way to worthiness. Instead of honoring my true self, I chased an illusion and bought a dress that only half covered me, along with a makeshift camisole to go under it. The result didn't look anything like the mannequin, nor did it feel like my imaginary ideal image. Nope. At the end of the day, I simply felt uncomfortably exposed, and the lace camisole was horribly itchy.

I had hoped to spend myself into worthiness, but all I did was reinforce my sense of worthlessness. The second time I wore the dress, a drunk woman at a wedding fell into me and spilled a giant glass of red wine down the right-hand side of it. After several different dry cleaners failed to remove the stain, I had to surrender to the fact that the dress was ruined, and so I continued to make payments for a year and a half for a tie-dyed burgundy and turquoise dress that never even fit me in the first place.

Even before the woman careened into me with her goblet of red wine, I knew I was a fraud. Even though I may have looked the part, I knew I wasn't the part. I spent money that I didn't even have in an attempt to buy my way to worthiness and ended up feeling more worthless than ever.

WHAT CAN YOU AFFORD TO SPEND?

It's pretty obvious that I couldn't afford the dress. By spending or giving away something you can't afford, whether it's money, time, energy, or self, you reinforce worthlessness. So it's important to know what you can afford, and sometimes the answer can be more complicated than in my dress example. To help you determine what you can afford, in the realm of money, I offer two guiding questions to consider.

> *By spending or giving away something you can't afford, whether it's money, time, energy, or self, you reinforce worthlessness.*

The first question to ask is: Can you pay cash? If you need to borrow money, use a credit card, take out an advance, or possibly bounce a check to be able to buy something, this technically means you cannot afford it, because you'd have to use money that you don't currently have to be able to make the purchase. If this is the case, you can't afford to spend the money.

The second question is: Will spending this money create negative consequences for you? Of course, there's no way to ever know what the future holds, but in general, most people have a pretty good idea of their typical income and expenses. If you're down to your last twenty bucks, then unnecessary spending is likely to create negative consequences for you. You might need that money for food, transportation to get you to your job, or a crucial unexpected expense. However, if you have a nice amount of savings and you know that you can spend the money without negatively impacting your life, then—as a general rule of thumb—this would mean you could afford it.

In my Gucci dress example, the answer was *no* to both questions. I couldn't pay cash, and even if I could, it would have created disastrous results for me and for my daughter. I wouldn't have been able to pay my rent, I wouldn't have been able to pay my utility bills, nor would I have been able to pay for groceries.

The dress example clearly illustrates that I couldn't afford to spend the money.

But this chapter is about something deeper and more profound than just spending money. It's about how and why you give away something that rightfully belongs to you. It's about how you spend your time, your energy, your attention, and your self and looking at this behavior as "what you give away."

This idea of parting with something that belongs to you is why I like to use the words *spending* and *giving* interchangeably. Sometimes, just substituting one word for the other helps change the way you perceive the behavior. For example, the opening line to this chapter was "Once upon a time, I spent a few thousand dollars on a Gucci dress."

What if I'd said it this way? "Once upon a time, I gave a few thousand dollars to Gucci for a dress." For me, using this language highlights the idea that I gave away something that was originally mine, and what I received in return definitely wasn't worth it, because it was so far outside the needs and priorities of my true self. This was the lesson that I had to learn time and time again as I began to accumulate self-worth. Rather than chase something that wasn't mine, that would never be mine, and that could never be mine (ideal image), I needed to learn to claim, own, caretake, and protect what was and had always been mine (true self).

Regardless of the currency, spending what you can't afford reinforces a sense of worthlessness. So when you consider giving or spending things like time, energy, and self, it's important to know how to determine whether you can afford to spend or give. To help you stay in the worthy cycle, I offer similar guiding questions to help you determine what you can afford to give away.

> *When you consider giving or spending things like time, energy, and self, it's important to know how to determine whether you can afford to spend or give.*

First, do you have an excess of resources to give or spend? This is kind of like the flight attendant's advice to put the oxygen mask on yourself first before you help others. Here, "an excess of resources" means that you have extra after you've cared for your*self* first. If you have to put yourself into debt in terms of your emotions, health, energy, or time, you can't afford to spend the resource. This means that before you give your time, your attention, your energy, or yourself to anyone or anything else, you first care for your true self. If you don't have extra to give, it means you can't afford it.

The second question to ask yourself to determine if you can afford to give or spend is: Will spending or giving this create negative consequences for you? Even when you're coming from a solid place of worthiness and caring for yourself, there will be times when giving or spending your excess may create an outcome that's harmful, difficult, or stressful. The idea here is to make a general determination about what might happen if you give the resource rather than save it. For example, if you're starting a new job, recovering from surgery, or having a difficult time with your partner, you may need to be more frugal with your resources and prioritize your time, energy, and attention for your current challenge rather than depleting yourself even further. Similar to being down to your last twenty bucks, the more limited your resources, the greater the negative impact when you spend them.

TWO TYPES OF SPENDING

When I bought the Gucci dress, I was looking at spending completely backward. Rather than focusing on what I was giving away (thousands of dollars over many months of future payments), I ignored what I already possessed and fixated on what I might possibly get (my ideal image).

This is a subtle difference, so let me say it again. Instead of seeing spending as *giving away a precious commodity that was in my care*, and rather than checking in to see if I could afford to spend or give away this precious commodity, I completely disregarded my asset and fixed my attention on *the illusion I hoped to acquire*. I saw spending as a means to an end rather than a giving away of something that I should protect.

And I didn't do this with just money. I did this with my time. I did this with my attention. I did this with my true self. I stopped focusing on what was rightfully mine and instead chased the illusion that I was trying to attain.

Regardless of what you're spending, whether it's money, time, energy, health, or self, I want you to frame it as giving away something that's in your care. This helps you focus on you and what you already possess before you move outward toward others or to your ideal image.

So let's look at two different types of spending: worthless and worthy. Worthless spending is the behavior of giving your money, time, attention, and energy to anything that prioritizes your ideal image over your true self. Worthless spending is giving away anything that you can't afford to give. When you're spending assets from an unworthy place, you inevitably reinforce a sense of worthlessness. Worthless stories influence behavior into worthless spending and giving, creating results that reinforce worthlessness.

The other type of spending is worthy spending. Worthy spending is the behavior of giving your money, time, attention, and energy to anything that prioritizes your true self over your ideal image. Worthy spending is investing in your true self. This type of spending always creates results that reinforce worthiness. When you're spending assets from a worthy place, you inevitably reinforce worthiness. Worthy stories influence behavior into worthy spending and giving, creating results that reinforce worthiness.

On the Gucci dress day, if I had honored my true self, I may have noticed how broken and raw I felt. Rather than try to run from those feelings, I may have just given permission to myself to feel them. Rather than spending my time and energy trying to pretend that everything was fine, I could have spent my time and energy being honest with my friends. And if I felt like I couldn't be honest with my friends, maybe I would have protected that sensitive self and removed her from a situation that seemed to reinforce a sense of worthlessness.

Rather than going shopping, I may have requested a different activity—one that would have reinforced a sense of worthiness. Rather than giving away my money (and many months of future money) to chase my ideal image, I may have abstained from buying something that didn't feel good and didn't fit correctly. From a place of worthiness, that day could have gone a thousand different ways. One thing is certain though—from a place of worthiness, a place where I respected and honored my true self, I would not have come home with that dress and camisole. I would not have come home in even more debt. And I would not have come home feeling even more worthless.

Often worthy spending means you give nothing away at all. Instead of giving away your money, time, attention, or energy, sometimes worthy spending means you save and you keep what is rightfully yours. Worthy spending is deliberate and conscious; it's an investment in your true self. It has a quality of being responsible instead of squandering your resources. There might even be a conscious sense of withholding or of taking care of something you love. There is a sense of protecting something valuable.

> Often worthy spending means you give nothing away at all. Instead of giving away your money, time, attention, or energy, sometimes worthy spending means you save and you keep what is rightfully yours.

GENEROSITY AND GIVING TO GET

But what about charity? What if you're spending or giving just to be generous? Does that make it a worthy spend?

The answer is not necessarily.

Regardless of the resource, whether you're giving money,

time, energy, or self, true generosity requires two things. First, the resource must be yours to give, meaning that you must have an excess of the resource to share. Second, for it to come from authentic generosity, there must be no strings attached and no alternative agenda.

When you give something you can't afford to give, even when you're doing so with the best of intentions, you end up deteriorating your self-worth rather than building it. This is important to understand, because many people overgive and overspend in the name of generosity. They think that by being generous, they will create a sense of worthiness. But this isn't how worthiness works. When you give something away that you don't own in the first place or that you can't afford to give, you end up reinforcing worthlessness rather than worthiness. Whether you're signing up to bring snacks for your daughter's volleyball team, or you feel obligated to go to your neighbor's barbecue, or you've been asked to cover someone's shift at work, first you need to check in with yourself to see if you can truly afford to give or spend the resource (time, energy, attention, money, self) necessary.

Start by asking yourself: Can I afford this? This means you'd have an excess of the resource to give and spend and that by doing so, you'd suffer no negative consequences. This means that you are able to give your time, attention, energy, and resources without creating stressful mental, emotional, physical, spiritual, or financial consequences for yourself.

When you come from a sense of worthiness, you care for your *self* first and then share what you can afford. True generosity requires that you caretake your assets, protect what's yours, and then give from overflow.

> *True generosity requires that you caretake your assets, protect what's yours, and then give from overflow.*

Next, you need to be very honest with yourself as to whether or not your so-called generosity has an agenda attached to it. If you're bringing snacks to the volleyball team because you don't want to look selfish, or if you're going to your neighbor's barbecue because you hope they come to your dinner party next week, or if you're covering a person's shift at work because you're hoping to get into your manager's good graces, this isn't generosity; this is a type of manipulation. It might be well-meaning manipulation, but it's still not coming from a worthy place. When you give to get, it's typically a behavior that's focused on your ideal image rather than on your true self. And any behavior that focuses on the ideal image ends up reinforcing the worthless cycle.

This doesn't mean that you shouldn't share, help, or give to others. Generosity is an important part of human connection; it helps to strengthen social bonds, and it's a fundamental aspect of worthiness. However, you must make self-care a priority so that you can truly give from a place of generosity. When you're coming from a place of overflow, where you have plenty of time, energy, and resources left over after you've cared for yourself, you'll be able to bring the snacks, go to the barbecue, and cover the shift.

WHAT DO YOU WANT?

If you'd asked me on the Gucci day to tell you what I really wanted, I probably would have said that I wanted the dress. But upon digging a little deeper, it's easy to see that I wanted the illusion of what I thought the dress would give me. In truth, I didn't *want* a dress that didn't cover my chest. I didn't *want* an itchy camisole. I didn't *want* to feel like a fraud. And I definitely didn't *want* to pay a credit card bill for a year and a half.

The truth is that I settled for something I didn't really want because I didn't believe I could have what I truly wanted. Security. Love. Worthiness. That's what I really wanted, but I didn't think that was actually possible. I was desperate, needy, and impatient. So I settled for the instant gratification of a cheaper, quicker substitute rather than investing my time, energy, and self into my true goals.

When you're considering how to give and spend your resources, I suggest starting by determining what you want. When I ask my students what they want, they typically start with dramatic fantasies: A yacht! A beach house! To win the lottery! My own private island!

Maybe you do want to give your time, money, and energy to a yacht. Maybe you do want to spend your time and energy caring for it, protecting it from storms, and repairing anything that goes wrong.

Maybe you really do want to give and spend your time, money, and energy to doing what it takes to buy a beach house. Maybe you do want to spend your time and energy going to the corner liquor store every single week to see if you can buy a winning lottery ticket. Maybe you do want to do what it takes to have that private island.

But after working with hundreds of students, I've found that most of us don't truly want the yacht or the private island, meaning that spending our time and energy doing what it takes to have these things wouldn't actually contribute to our self-worth.

> *To build self-worth, you need to know what you really want, and you also need to be willing to spend and give what it takes to create it.*

To build self-worth, you need to know what you really want, and you also need to be willing to spend and give what it takes to create it. Rather than focusing on a potential outcome, you take a more holistic approach and focus on the entire journey. So I want you to just take a few moments to think about what you really want. But rather than thinking about what you'd like to get, focus on how you want to spend and give, what you want to invest in.

What do you want to give your time and energy to? How do you want to spend your resources?

Do you want a loving relationship? If so, you'd need to be willing to spend and give your time, energy, and attention toward creating a loving relationship.

Do you want to have a strong and healthy body? If so, you'd need to be willing to spend and give your time, energy, and attention toward doing what it takes to have a healthy body.

Do you want to write a book? Become a star on Broadway? Build a house near the water? Sail to Alaska? If so, you'd need to be willing to spend and give your time, energy, and attention toward doing what it takes to make these outcomes a reality.

"What do you want?" isn't always an easy question to answer, but when you spend time with this question, it often leads to profound insights.

In class, I have students create a list. At the top of the page, they write *I want to spend and give my time, attention, and energy to* and then they list twenty things. For each of the twenty things, they must be willing to spend their time, attention, and energy doing what it takes to create this desired outcome.

So far, no one has had a yacht or a private island on their list. Usually they have things like weekly family dinner, regular date nights with a spouse, get more rest, read more books. Better communication with a partner. More in-real-life friends.

Learn to cook a plant-based diet. Learn to meditate. Daily self-care practice.

You might find that you've trained yourself out of having this conversation because you don't want to be disappointed. So instead of focusing on what you want, you've learned to settle for what you think you might be able to get. This is common, yet it only reinforces worthlessness. The work here is to stretch beyond your habitual worthless stories and reach for desires that honor your true self.

For example, maybe you really want to move. And maybe you don't simply want to move from one side of town to the other, but you actually want to move from one side of the state to the other. This desire might seem so outlandish, so selfish, so risky, that you might not even allow yourself to think it. Maybe your kids are happy at their schools. Maybe your partner has a steady job. In a case like this, it's common to feel guilty, ungrateful, or even selfish to think of uprooting your family. This secret inner desire can quickly become squelched by a laundry list of responsibilities and justifications for why you just need to tough it out and stay put.

Yet looking through the lens of what you are willing to give your time and energy to, you might see the move in a different way. Rather than seeing the end result—a new house in a new place (something that you really can't even fathom)—you can focus on what would be necessary for the entire journey. You could imagine visiting the town you hope to live in, you could look online for houses, and you could dream about having coffee in your new kitchen. You could envision boxing up your house, hiring movers, and all the tiny details that would go into making the move a reality. You could imagine finding new schools for your kids, a new job for your partner. You could imagine sorting out the details of new doctors, new dentists, new grocery stores, and new gas stations. Rather than seeing the move as an end result you hope to get—something that seems impossible to have—you could see it as an entire process you want to invest in, something you have a hand in creating.

Inevitably, there will be things on your list that seem difficult or even downright unattainable. So the next step is to give permission to yourself, to directly state that you are allowed to give your time and energy to these things. You give yourself permission to want it. You honor and respect the desire for it.

On your paper, you could write *Move across the state*, and next to it in all caps write *YOU ARE ALLOWED TO WANT THAT.* Meaning that you are allowed to want to look online for houses. You are allowed to visit the town. You are allowed to dream about cozy mornings in your new kitchen. You are allowed to come up with a plan for boxing up your house. You are allowed to want all of it. You are allowed to spend and give yourself to this pursuit.

Your perception changes in a profound way when you realize that wanting to give your time and energy to something hurts no one. And rather than waiting for a permission slip to fall from the sky, you are allowed to just want what you want.

Now it's your turn. I want you to make a list of twenty different things that you want to *give* your energy to or *spend* your resources on. These do not have to be things that cost money.

These do not have to be things that you don't already have. In fact, some of the most important things on your list might be things that you've already invested in. Whether you're trying to create something new or you're deeply grateful for something you have, this is an exercise to help you integrate the idea that what you give deserves your attention and respect.

The mantra for this exercise is *I have permission to give my energy to this. I have permission to want this.* Honor what you want, and reinforce your worthiness by showing that *your wishes to give and spend* are worth your time and your attention.

WORTHY WORK: YOUR NEXT MEAL

Take a picture of your next meal or snack exactly as it looks before you eat it. Don't wait for the day that you cook a candlelit five-course meal. Don't wait for when you're at a fancy restaurant and you have a perfectly plated meal in front of you. Don't wait for a meal that fits your rules about what you deem healthy, good, nutritious, or socially correct. This isn't about trying to create a Pinterest-worthy picture. It's about taking an honest look at how you spend and give when it comes to feeding yourself.

As I said before, I recommend using a photograph because we tend to become blind to the little details in our lives, and a photo can help us take an inventory that's more accurate. So whether your next meal is at your desk at work, at the dining room table, or in your car on your way to pick up your kids from school, just take a quick snapshot of the scene.

When I'm looking at my students' meal photos, I'm not

only looking at what they are eating. I'm also looking at where they are eating. I'm looking at the dishes or lack of dishes. I'm looking at the presentation or care that goes into their food. I'm looking for any clue that reinforces a sense of worthiness or worthlessness.

I'm not necessarily looking for healthy food or cooked food or whether there's a napkin. I'm looking at how they give to themselves. Worthiness means that you give and you spend generously to yourself for yourself. Sometimes that looks like a plate of broccoli and grilled chicken. Sometimes that looks like a cookie in the passenger seat of your car. This isn't about food rules or about fancy cuisine; this is more about the small and invisible ways that we don't allow ourselves to have what we truly want and need. This is about the unconscious ways that we settle for less than we deserve, thereby reinforcing a sense of worthlessness.

To give you an idea of how this works, let me share a few examples.

REAL STORIES: ANGELA

Angela, a high school counselor and mother of two teenagers, signed up for my class to help her end her struggle with her body. Always smiling and genuinely kind, I could see why high school students would love her. Outwardly, she was friendly and outgoing. But toward herself, she was ruthless. She shared, "Everything depends on what the scale says that day. I am meticulous with counting calories. I measure out every meal. And if the scale doesn't reflect what I want, I go into perfectionistic overdrive. I mentally berate myself and physically punish myself by withholding food." Historically, she'd thought her self-worth was related to her weight, and she hoped to break that cycle. When I studied Angela's meal photo, it was much like I'd expected. Everything was a little too perfect. The photo showed a white linen place mat and a white cloth napkin on what appeared to be a black, high-gloss dining room table. In the center was a large white plate with steamed spinach and a small piece of salmon, with a full place setting—two forks, a knife, a spoon. A crystal glass of sparkling water sat on the upper right-hand corner of the place mat. It seemed that she had an ideal image that she was trying to attain, either through the perfect food or the perfect place setting. Nothing seemed real or lived in except for the plate, which was chipped along the edge in two places.

I asked Angela to share what she saw in the photo. She said, "I see someone who is trying to do it all right. To be honest, I took four different photos this week before I posted one. I kept finding something wrong with the meal, and I didn't want you to criticize it. I want to show you how hard I try to be healthy. I don't want to look like someone with a weight problem."

I could sense how exposed and vulnerable Angela felt and how hard she was trying to do everything right. I wanted to inquire in a way that would help her find answers from her true self, and I knew that I needed to show extra care so as not to offend or threaten her ideal image. So I asked her to give me a description of everything she saw in the photo.

She said, "I see someone who is trying really hard. I don't

even know if spinach and salmon is the right meal. I don't even know if sparkling water is the right drink. Every single time I eat something, I can find a rule that I'm breaking, and I don't even know what to eat anymore. I like that I went through the extra steps to set up a nice place setting, even though I hate those dishes. My mother gave them to me as a college graduation gift, and I've been living with them ever since."

"Was the meal good? Do you like salmon and spinach?" I asked.

She said no but that she ate it because it's healthy.

When I asked if this photo showed a reinforcement of worthiness or a reinforcement of worthlessness, Angela said it made her feel worthless. It was food that she didn't even like, served on a plate that she feels like she's just supposed to live with.

When you look at this meal through the lens of giving and spending, she gave an enormous amount of time and energy toward her ideal image and very little to the real Angela. To shift into the worthy cycle, she'd need to change at least one small thing to honor, respect, and care for her true self. Angela decided to break out of her idea of perfection by limiting the power of her rules and allowing herself permission to relax at mealtime. Instead of seeing meals as something she needed to get "right," she needed to start with honoring what she truly wanted. As a visual representation of breaking rules to honor her true self, she decided to retire the old white plates and replace them with ones that made her smile. She found six different plates—all different colors, all different sizes, nothing matching.

She posted her after photo a few days later, which showed a peanut butter and jelly sandwich on an emerald-green glass plate along with a can of Diet Coke. She wrote, "This picture simply looks like freedom. I might not eat like this all the time, but it feels so good to just put my rules aside and allow myself to relax. This meal was the yummiest thing I've eaten in weeks, and the Diet Coke was a guilty pleasure and so worth it."

REAL STORIES: KIM

Kim, a human resources director, an avid cat lover, and happily single after ending her fifteen-year marriage, signed up for my class because she tended to overwork to the point of exhaustion. She shared that her self-worth was deeply tied to her job performance, and she lacked any energy for self-care. She said, "Now that I live alone, I have a difficult time knowing when to say no. I end up running myself into the ground before I realize that I've taken on too much." The first thing I noticed when I looked at Kim's photo was that it appeared to be taken quickly, from within her cubicle at work. It was a little out of focus, and nothing about the photo looked contrived or posed. It looked like she took a photo of her desk exactly as it was in that moment. It didn't seem like Kim had tried to make things appear perfect; rather the picture looked like a true representation of a typical workday meal. I could see part of her desktop computer, a vertical filing system, and a gray cubicle wall. Scattered across her desk were a bunch of reports, spreadsheets, and papers. Her meal was on top of the papers: a protein bar, a plastic smoothie shaker holding some sort of liquid, and a paper cup of coffee.

When I asked her about her photo, she shared, "This is how I eat almost every meal. I grab something convenient and keep working. I never take a lunch break, and I always work through dinner. You can't see it here in this photo, but in my file drawer, I have a box of protein bars and instant shake packets. I'm so sick of eating like this, but I can't figure out a way to leave my desk once I'm at work, and I'd rather just get through the day."

When asked if this picture reinforced worthiness or worthlessness, she said, "I think there's a bit of both. In one way, I can see that I'm pretty comfortable with showing this aspect of my life. I didn't stress out about it, nor did I try to stage the photo. But I do think there's room for growth here. I'd like to show more self-care, and I'd like to spend more time and energy on nourishing myself in ways that reinforce worthiness."

She had several ideas for little things she might consider changing: ordering tasty takeout, eating outside once a week, or going into the employee lounge at lunch. Yet these ideas seemed to fall flat and didn't really inspire her to want to change. I asked her, "What do you really want? How do you really want to spend your time and energy?" She smiled and instantly had an idea. She said she's always loved the idea of a bento box—she loved organization, and she loved the idea of offering herself kindness, creativity, and something beautiful at lunch.

When she posted her after picture, the photo still showed the backdrop of a cubicle and a desk, yet now, on top of the paperwork was a neatly organized little bento box with colorful, fresh food that she'd made for herself the previous evening. To move into the worthy cycle, Kim didn't need to change every single thing about the way she worked or her meal habits. She didn't even need to leave her cubicle. She simply needed to show a little care and respect for her true self. Worthy work is about taking one small step to reinforce a sense of worthiness. Kim chose to give herself something she loved: color, beauty, and fresh food right there at her desk. Rather than ripping open a stale protein packet, she now had a visual reinforcement of her own sense of worthiness.

REAL STORIES: MELISSA

Melissa signed up for my class to try to understand why her marriage was struggling. A Midwestern young woman with traditional values, she shared that the more she tried to be the perfect wife, the less her husband wanted to be home. They had only been married a few short years, and she was afraid that they'd already drifted apart. She said, "I'd always thought that if you had a beautiful home and good food, people would just want to be there. But the more effort I give, the more I seem to push him away." The first thing I noticed in Melissa's meal picture was her gorgeous dining room table. The long planks of restored wood looked cozy and inviting. The meal was beautiful: a large salad bowl in the middle flanked by a plate of steaming grilled chicken. There were two place settings, his and hers, a bottle of wine, cloth napkins.

When I asked her about her photo, she shared, "This is

what I do every night. I spend an enormous amount of time and energy cooking a beautiful meal. And then I sit and wait for my husband to come home before I eat. Most nights, I end up eating well after the food is cold. Most nights, I just end up pissed off."

When asked if this picture reinforced worthiness or worthlessness, she said, "If this meal were just for me, I think it would reinforce worthiness. But I feel like a jerk when I just cook for myself. The least I can do is to make enough for both of us. So I'm guessing that this is probably me reinforcing worthlessness."

Even though she spoke with a tinge of embarrassment and frustration, she rolled her eyes and threw her hands up in the air. She still had a sense of humor.

So I challenged her to take an after picture that had nothing to do with home, nothing to do with her marriage, and nothing to do with her ideal image. "If no one was looking and this meal was only for you, what would you give to your precious self?"

The following day, she posted her after picture. In the center of the photo was Melissa's hand holding a large chocolate chip cookie. I could see that she was in her car and that beyond the windows was a serene landscape of lake and sky. She shared, "I did it. I did something just for me. I went to the bakery and bought myself a cookie, and then I took the long way home and stopped at the edge of my favorite lake and watched the sun go down. I can't believe how different I feel. I can't believe how long it has taken me to do something like this."

Through small changes, like Angela's green plate, Kim's colorful lunch, and Melissa's long route home, each of these women learned that the way they spend and give deserves their time and attention. And by taking deliberate action to honor their true selves, they reinforced their own worthiness. This is how self-worth is built.

YOUR WORTHY WORK

Very important: Under no circumstances are you allowed to do this exercise with the intention of self-shaming, adding to your to-do list, or causing yourself overwhelming shame spirals or anxiety. This exercise is only to be done with compassion and love.

Now it's your turn. Take a look at the photo of your meal with your detective eye. In the photo, do you see any evidence of how you give and spend your time, energy, and resources? Do you see any evidence of how you're not giving or spending time, energy, or resources? What do you notice? Do you see any evidence that may be reinforcing a worthless story?

You're looking for clues of where there's a disregard for your true self. This might look like eating things you don't love or eating in an atmosphere that doesn't nourish you. This might look like not feeding yourself enough or not allowing yourself enough time to eat. You're also looking for clues of where you glorify the importance of the ideal image. You're looking at whether you see evidence that reinforces worthiness or evidence that reinforces worthlessness.

You affirm your own worthiness when you spend and give in a way that reinforces that you are worth your own time, attention, and care. Do you see any evidence of this in your picture?

Once you've taken a good look at your photo, the next step is to determine one small change that you can make today that strengthens the idea that your true self is valuable. What small change can you make to help reinforce a sense of worthiness? This means that you deliberately do something that reinforces that you are worth your own time, attention, and energy.

Now go do that thing and take an action that reinforces worthiness. Do something that reminds you that you deserve your own respect and attention.

JOURNALING PROMPTS

1. Historically, which of your resources do you tend to over-give or overspend? What type of consequences has this created in your life?

2. Think of a time when you felt like you had an excess of resources to share. What was going on in your life at that time? How did it feel?

3. Where in your life do you need to be more conservative with your resources? What will you gain by saving rather than overgiving?

CHAPTER 4
Receiving and Earning

You never know when you're about to learn something that will completely change your life. You never know who your teacher is going to be or where the lesson will occur. However, if you're paying attention, you'll find worthiness teachers all around you. My biggest lesson about earning and receiving didn't come from my accountant or my financial advisor. It didn't come via a spreadsheet or a financial statement or even from a monetary transaction. My biggest lesson happened at the checkout stand in a random grocery store.

Let me paint you a picture of my life at that point in time. This was about eight years after the Gucci dress incident, after which I'd stopped compulsively shopping and had completely paid off my debt. My business had grown well beyond a private coaching practice. By that time, I was running several retreats per year all over the United States. Additionally, I had a team of teachers who were helping me run large training programs. I was typically working twelve-hour days, seven days a week, and I'd been working like this for a solid three years.

Even though I'd gotten myself out of debt, I still seemed to hover just under a financial ceiling that I couldn't break through. The more money the business made, the more money the business cost. Travel expenses, teacher expenses, insurance, and taxes ate up the majority of the income, and I just kept treading financial water, staying in the same place year after year. Teachers were always paid first, then retreat costs for locations, then all other business expenses. After everything was paid, I lived on whatever was left over. But there was hardly ever anything left over. There was always something that came up or someone else who needed to be paid. Or another marketing opportunity to invest in. Or a new location to lock down for a retreat. My business had become complicated and unwieldy—not only financially but also in how much I was trying to manage. I wasn't just a coach anymore. I managed teams of teachers, retreat locations, my own retreat center, weekly in-person classes, dozens of weekly online classes, two websites, and a growing list of students. I needed more help, but I couldn't afford it. I needed to advertise more, but I couldn't afford to dump more money into the advertising budget. I was on a treadmill, working harder than I've ever worked and barely breaking even. Throughout my business and in several areas of my life, I was hustling, working, trying, giving, and spending everything I had.

I was in a critical place—physically exhausted, emotionally and financially spent. I'd just returned from leading a retreat in Vermont where I'd had a significant health scare and had spent weeks in bed trying to recover. My teachers were being paid well, my students were receiving quality coaching, and yet personally, quietly, secretly, I was struggling to make ends meet at home. I had no debt and minimal expenses, but no matter how much I cut back, I only had just enough to get by. Every expense was calculated as I waited to make sure I had enough after everyone was paid. My daughter and I were at the end of the money line, and most months, my personal bank account hovered right around zero.

Which is why I happened to be in the grocery store with my assistant, Kristi. I'd called an emergency team retreat, on location in California. I rented a large house for the weekend and invited all the teachers who worked for me.

As my team boarded airplanes and made their way to the central coast of California, Kristi and I went to the grocery store to stock the vacation rental with healthy snacks, loads of bubbly waters, and tons of good coffee. At the checkout stand, the items slid across the conveyor belt as Kristi and I talked a mile a minute about all the items on the roster for our team retreat weekend. Rather than having systems and policies in place, there were aspects of my business that had simply been held together by the glue of my own overachiever efforts. And that would no longer work—my boss-lady mojo had been knocked out of me in Vermont. I needed some tough love. I needed fresh eyes on the problem. I'd hoped that my team might be able to help come up with new strategies that would help save the business in a way that didn't require more and more of my time, effort, attention, and financial capital.

I paid the checker, and Kristi and I waited while the bagger finished loading our groceries back into our cart. When he loaded the last paper bag, it split and began to rip down the side seam. Now, pause. I need to slow this moment down, because a lot happened in the span of just a few seconds.

I saw the bag rip. I saw the grocery clerk place the ripped bag into the cart. I knew he had seen the rip. He knew he'd placed a heavy bag with a tear threatening to progress down the side and looked at both of us with a slightly apologetic "Oh well" look on his face. And for just a second, a familiar feeling of disappointment and exhaustion washed over me as I made a mental note to remember which bag was ripped so that we didn't end up with a bagful of tangerines and apples rolling down the driveway at the retreat house. In other words, I started strategizing about how I would need to spend more of my time, energy, and attention to protect the groceries. On top of everything else I had on my mind, I'd simply add another item—note to self: be careful with this ripped bag. Note to self: make sure that you personally unload the ripped bag, because Kristi might forget. Note to self: those apples and tangerines will roll away if the bag rips more. Note to self: don't forget which bag is faulty.

So that all happened within about two and a half seconds before Kristi did something radical. Unbelievable, really.

She turned to the grocery clerk and said, "Oh no, that bag is ripped. Could you double bag it?"

Her question stopped me in my tracks. It was such a small thing for Kristi—I could tell that this was second nature for her. She didn't seem apologetic, nor did she seem unkind. She was simply making a reasonable request. Yet this request highlighted a huge problem within me. Up until that moment, it hadn't even occurred to me that I could or should ask for help. It hadn't even occurred to me that this wasn't asking for a favor; it was merely the act of protecting what was rightfully mine. I had paid for the groceries, and I had paid the extra ten cents each for the bags. And rather than honoring my time, money, and efforts, instead my knee-jerk response was to give and spend more of myself in this tiny way. Rather than seeing that someone could or would meet me halfway, I took it upon myself to simply make up the difference.

I had thought that I'd mastered spending because I had gotten myself out of financial debt, but there was so much more to this behavior that I'd missed. I was still massively over-spending my time, energy, and self. I was also missing a crucial piece of the puzzle because I had no clear boundary for what I expected in return. I was willing to spend everything and receive nothing. You know the saying, "Give them an inch and they'll take a mile"? Well, my worthless story was something like the exact opposite of that. If you gave me an inch, I'd walk five hundred miles.

Maybe you are completely comfortable asking for a bag at the grocery checkout. If so, stay with me, because this issue might not show up for you at the checkout stand. It might manifest in your romantic life (or lack of), in your relationship with your kids, or at work. Once you know what to look for, you may be surprised to find how often you settle for underearning and under-receiving and how these habits are keeping you stuck at a lower worthiness ceiling than you deserve.

> *Once you know what to look for, you may be surprised to find how often you settle for underearning and under-receiving.*

I offer this example primarily because it's an almost humorous illustration of just how far down the unworthiness hole I had fallen, how little I was willing to settle for, and how shocking it was for me to see a different behavior modeled. When Kristi spoke those words, I swiveled my head in her direction, eyes wide open and mouth gaping, and stood there, completely stunned.

The grocery clerk smiled and said, "Sure." He took out another bag and double bagged the ripped one before placing it back into our cart. For him, this was no big deal.

I wish I could say that I felt comfortable with this transaction, but I didn't. I looked at the people behind me in line and smiled apologetically. I hunched my shoulders, trying to make myself a little smaller, trying to look as nice and as kind as possible. I didn't want anyone to be mad at me for taking up extra time. I didn't want anyone to think I was selfish or entitled. Without even realizing it, I had already decided that I was willing to give away my own time and energy so that I could portray my ideal image to strangers—a nice, generous woman who would never hold up the line. A woman who could do all the things and never get tired, never need help. A woman who just handled things. A woman who would hold the damned bag together without blinking. I was willing to overspend resources and ask for nothing in return, because frankly, I just wanted a few strangers to like me.

Kristi's simple request was a stark contrast to my own reaction, and I could see that this whole process of forgoing my needs to be more likable wasn't a small thing—it was a chronic and worthless habit. And it wasn't just happening at the checkout stand. I had called an emergency team retreat because this was happening everywhere in my life, my business, my health, my money. If I had an unhappy client, I'd give them more time and attention. If I had a team member who wasn't pulling their weight, I'd overcompensate by picking up the slack. I made sure everyone else was paid well even when that meant that I was averaging far less than minimum wage for my own time. At that point, when I saw a problem, I automatically strategized about how to spend and give more of myself. I was metaphorically up to my eyeballs in ripped grocery bags, exhausted from trying to juggle runaway fruit baskets, and manically doing it all with a smile so as not to tarnish my ideal image.

It never occurred to me that I should require more from my business. It never occurred to me that I should ask for more from anyone or anything. I was sacrificing myself at the altar of my ideal image, trying to arrive at what I'd hoped would be a feeling of worthiness. But overspending and underearning, whether we're talking about money, love, attention, or self, only ever leads to worthlessness.

Rather than protecting what was rightfully mine, I had given away my time, my energy, my money, and my *self* in service of my ideal image. But life had given me a few hard knocks, and by the time I called the emergency team retreat, that ideal image had lost much of its power. Vanity and arrogance had been knocked right out of me. I had no more fight. I had been humbled, and I knew I needed to surrender.

To break through my self-inflicted worthiness ceiling, I would be required to ask for more. I would need to learn how to receive more. I would need to earn what I deserved rather than settling for less. And I would need to get specific about what I expected in return for what I spent and gave.

I wasn't even aware of the worthless story that had been driving this behavior, that had kept me stuck in a worthless cycle. For most of my life, I had done everything in my power to be an asset rather than a liability. This started early in my childhood—trying to need less, want less, and ask for less. In return, I had hoped to render myself more lovable. I had lived most of my life trying to be an asset to everyone—always adding value, always giving more of myself, always spending everything I had in hopes that I would be loved. In hopes that I would belong. In hopes that I would be safe.

This strategy worked well as a child in a dysfunctional family unit. I learned that if I picked up the slack for my parents, they were kinder to me. I learned that if I never asked for anything, they wouldn't push me away. But this habit created disastrous results for me in my adult life. Rather than meet someone halfway, I'd run the full distance and then some. I'd watch their kids, cook them dinner, rub their feet, or bring them presents. I'd make myself indispensable. Without realizing it, I believed that I could make myself so useful to them that they'd have to tolerate me. I'd make myself so important to them that they wouldn't be able to abandon me, reject me, or hate me.

I did this with men. I did this with family. I did this with my students. I did this with friends. Always trying to hide any needs, any requirements, any vulnerabilities, while painting myself as having an abundance of resources to generously offer.

I would fill in the blank spots with any relationship; if anything was missing, I'd take care of it. I thought this was what love was made of: the continual act of picking up the slack in someone else's life. And of course, with this strategy, you tend to attract the same type of person over and over. I used to joke with my girlfriends, "Give me a man with a decent job, and I'll turn them into a broke loser who can't pay the rent." That line always got a good laugh, because it was true—several times over. If I took care of them, paid their rent, or made them dinner, I'd never have to know if they really loved me or wanted me. Rather than creating boundaries around what I required in return, I'd simply keep spending more and giving more—preventing me from ever having to know how someone really felt about me. Preventing me from ever having to face whether they believed I was worthy. Preventing me from ever realizing that I alone held the key to my own worth.

BOUNDARIES AND FAIR COMPENSATION

Whether we are talking about the worthy cycle or the worthless cycle, the three points of the cycle include the story, the behavior, and the reinforcement of the story. As I shared before, the best way to move out of worthlessness and into the worthy cycle is to change your behavior. In this chapter, we are specifically looking at the behavior of earning and receiving.

When I talk about earning and receiving, I want you to look at this particular aspect of behavior through a lens of what you require, what you expect, or what you ask for in return for your spending and giving. Rather than overspending and underearning, which diminish your worth, worthiness requires clear and conscious boundaries around your spending and earning.

> Rather than overspending and underearning, which diminish your worth, worthiness requires clear and conscious boundaries around your spending and earning.

Boundaries are not complaints, threats, or ultimatums. They aren't mean, cruel, or rude. They are simply clear communication of what's true for you, helping others know who you are and how to interact with you. A boundary can be a firm line in the sand or a very subtle shift. When we are clear with our boundaries, no one who meets us, works with us, or tries to emotionally connect with us is left guessing.

Boundaries are not about trying to make someone else change. Instead, you state your request and wait. Sometimes you're lucky and the person hears your request and honors it immediately. But this isn't always the case. Sometimes you'll state your request, and it isn't honored at all. Sometimes the other person doesn't want what you want. Sometimes the other person won't respect your needs or wishes. And that's okay. It's not their job to honor your worth—it's yours. When someone doesn't respect your desires, your wishes, or your requests, you will probably have to be the one to take the necessary action to protect and restore the boundary.

> *When someone doesn't respect your desires, your wishes, or your requests, you will probably have to be the one to take the necessary action to protect and restore the boundary.*

By settling for less than you deserve, whether we're talking about money, time, attention, or something else, you reinforce your own worthlessness. So it's important to know what you deserve to earn or receive. Rather than thinking about earning and receiving as something that just happens to come your way, I want you to see it more as something that you ask for, that you require, or that you expect in return.

In the last chapter, I talked about spending being determined by what you can afford. When you spend more than you can afford, it's called overspending. In this chapter, the flip side—earning—is determined by how much you need to receive in return for what you give. This is what you need to sustain and strengthen yourself. To build worth, whether we are talking about financial worth or self-worth, you need to earn enough to support yourself and protect your resources.

To help you determine how much you need to earn, in the realm of money, I offer one guiding question to consider:

Is this fair compensation? You are the only one who can answer this question. It has nothing to do with the marketplace or what the going rate is for your particular service or product; rather, this is about what you give in exchange for what you receive. When you settle for unfair compensation, you set yourself up for an outcome that's unsustainable. This means you're either overgiving or under-receiving, and over time, this cycle depletes your resources, and your financial worth declines until eventually you bottom out. This is what happens when you settle for less than you deserve. This is what happened to me (by my own hand, mind you). I over-worked and underpaid myself, and after three years, I had no reserves left. My energy, my time, my health, and my money had been completely exhausted.

Fair compensation, however, *is* sustainable. When you receive back equal or more than you give, you gain resources over time and gradually increase your reserves. To turn my business around, I needed to move in the direction of sustainability. This meant that I had to require fair compensation for myself. To fix this problem, I would need to give less, meaning that I'd need to set boundaries with myself and stop myself from giving more than I was being compensated for. And I would have to earn more in return for what I was giving away, meaning that I'd need to require more in exchange for my efforts. In other words, I needed to work less and earn more.

This wasn't simply a money problem. It was larger and more profound than that. The truth was that I was underearning—settling for less than I deserved—in almost every aspect of my life, a behavior that constantly reinforced a sense of worthlessness.

So when I talk about earning, I start with money to show you the basics. But I also want to apply these lessons to the broader sense of what you receive in exchange for your time, energy, attention, kindness, and love. Regardless of the currency, settling for unfair compensation always reinforces a sense of worthlessness. So when you consider earning or receiving things like time, energy, attention, and respect, it's important to know how to determine how much you require. To help you stay in the worthy cycle, I offer you the same guiding question, seen through a different lens, to help you determine what you need to ask for, require, and expect.

> *Regardless of the currency, settling for unfair compensation always reinforces a sense of worthlessness.*

Is this fair compensation? Similar to how this works with regard to money, fair compensation can also be considered for any exchange of giving and receiving. Whether you are exchanging time, attention, energy, or love, unfair compensation sets you up for an outcome that's unsustainable. When you're overgiving, under-receiving, or both, over time, your resources are depleted, your self-worth declines, and eventually you bottom out. Fair compensation, however, creates the opposite: a sustainable outcome where you gain resources over time and increase your reserves.

In the double-grocery-bag scenario, I had paid in full for my groceries and bags. Fair compensation would require receiving a bag that did its job. Kristi knew this and easily asked for it. My knee-jerk reaction had been to settle for unfair compensation, thereby adding to an unsustainable lifestyle where I continued to deplete more and more of my limited resources (time, energy, attention).

Similarly, in romantic relationships, I had repeatedly created situations where I'd become both the servant and the bank. In return, all I had asked for was to simply be tolerated.

This wasn't fair compensation, and it created an unsustainable outcome. Which brings up a difficult question. When it comes to a relationship, what does one deserve?

FAIR COMPENSATION WITH RELATIONSHIPS

When we are talking about earning and receiving within a relationship, it's a little more complicated than simply talking about earning and receiving fair compensation for a product or service.

Now this can get a little tricky, because fair compensation in relationships can easily be confused with tit for tat or keeping score, neither of which fosters intimacy and trust or reinforces a sense of worthiness. When considering fair compensation within a relationship, the key is to focus on whether *your own* behavior is sustainable or whether you are depleting your resources. The essential word here is *you*. This strategy requires that you maintain healthy boundaries by modifying your own behavior so as not to overgive and under-receive.

> When considering fair compensation within a relationship, the key is to focus on whether your own behavior is sustainable.

Tit for tat is different. It's a strategy focused on retaliation. That is when you focus on the other person's behavior and seek to punish, manipulate, or exact vengeance to get them to change. This is reactive rather than proactive, and the focus is on the other person. This strategy doesn't have boundaries, and you try to change the other's behavior rather than focusing on your own. As a general rule of thumb, keep your eyes on your own paper when it comes to earning and receiving.

For example, to change your relationship, you might have to learn a blunt and simple truth: to contain yourself. Healthy boundaries work in two different ways—one is to protect you from the outside in, and the other is to protect you from the inside out. Think of it this way: walls can only protect you if you stay *inside* the house. In your relationships, you might run around putting out fires and do anything but stay within your own walls. So your personal work would be to learn to keep yourself inside your boundary line and wait. This is extremely uncomfortable, and it means that rather than jumping up to help someone, you'd have to wait to see if they helped themselves. You'd have to learn to be patient, and this will feel intensely vulnerable—excruciating, really. Rather than repeatedly calling or texting to keep a conversation alive, you'll have to wait to see how often *they* naturally want to engage with you. Rather than automatically paying for a meal, you'll wait to see how *they* want to handle it. Rather than changing your schedule, you'd meet at times that worked for *both* of you. Rather than trying to shape-shift yourself into something that they might want, you'll have to wait to figure out if they are someone who you want. By taking a step back and containing your overgiving, you'll be able to see a potential partner more clearly. Rather than filling in the blanks, you'll learn to wait to see if you are a good fit.

TWO TYPES OF EARNING

At the time of the double-bagging fiasco, I looked at earning completely backward. Rather than seeing earning as a requirement to receive what was rightfully mine (fair compensation), I ignored my own needs and focused on what I might possibly be given. I viewed earning as something that just kind of landed on me, or as something that happened sometimes, or as some kind of wish to be granted by the universe, by fate, or by a fairy godmother. I thought my earning potential was in someone else's hands. I didn't realize that it was determined by me and me alone.

Of course, I had this wrong in all areas of my life, not just with money. Instead of seeing earning and receiving as a boundary issue and my own responsibility, I saw it as a bad luck issue, where it seemed like I just couldn't catch a break. I wasn't only waiting for a magical paycheck to arrive, I was also waiting for someone to give me a day off, for someone to swoop in and love me, for someone to help me rest. I didn't focus on the precious assets that I had given away, whether that had been my time, my energy, my health, or my love. And I certainly didn't know that I could or that I should require fair compensation for what I'd given away.

Regardless of what you're spending and giving, I want

you to see earning and receiving as something you rightfully deserve. This helps you focus on you first, so that you determine your line for fair compensation.

> *Regardless of what you're spending and giving, I want you to see earning and receiving as something you rightfully deserve.*

So let's look at two different types of earning: worthless and worthy. Worthless earning is settling for unfair compensation. Worthless earning is unsustainable and depletes your resources. Worthless earning is receiving less than you rightfully deserve. This type of earning always creates results that reinforce worthlessness.

The other type of earning is worthy earning. Worthy earning is the requirement of fair compensation. Worthy earning is sustainable and increases your resources. Worthy earning is receiving what you rightfully deserve. This type of earning always creates results that reinforce worthiness. When you're earning assets from a worthy place, you inevitably reinforce worthiness. Worthy stories influence behavior into worthy earning and receiving, creating results that reinforce worthiness.

Worthy earning is built on a foundation of healthy boundaries, and healthy boundaries start with honoring, respecting, and caring for your true self. This means that you clearly define what will be sustainable for you. This means that you figure out what will support you, what will sustain you, and what will stop your resources from becoming depleted.

For example, if you notice that you seem to give your time away too freely, you set a boundary with yourself around time. You give a little time and then wait to see if you receive back fair compensation. This doesn't mean that you spend two hours doing something for someone and that they spend two hours doing something for you. Rather, it means that you figure out what you'd need to receive in exchange for those two hours to sustain yourself and to protect your resources.

Maybe this means that you agree to spend all evening helping your teenage son build a diorama for his history project, and in return, you ask him to engage and participate in the process rather than zoning out on his phone. This doesn't necessarily mean that you'll receive what you're asking for, but you will have set a clear boundary for what you are willing to spend and what you expect in return. Therefore, if you're busy gluing miniature trees while he grabs his phone, lies down on the couch, and turns on Netflix, you then modify your behavior and stop yourself from continuing to give and spend your resources. Without blame, without shame, without finger wagging, you simply remove yourself and allow him to experience the natural consequences of his own behavior. This might mean that he gets a zero for an unfinished project. Or it might mean that he's up all night working on it by himself. It might even mean that he gets mad at you for not enabling his poor behavior. But here's the deal: if you want to build self-worth (and teach your kids to do the same), it's up to you to honor your own boundaries. Rather than trying to create a quick fix by giving more of yourself away, you may just have to sit on your hands and count to ten to stop yourself from grabbing that damned glue gun.

Here's another example: maybe you take the risk to share a vulnerable subject with a friend, and in return, you expect her to listen without interrupting. To set a boundary, you must clearly communicate your request to the other person. You can do this during the course of the conversation, by text, or even by sticky note. You can ask for this upfront by saying, "I have something vulnerable to share with you, and I'd love to have you listen before commenting." She may or may not honor your request. No matter what course of action she takes, her behavior is crucial feedback. If she honors your request, it will likely create calm within the relationship, a sustainable sense of equality and balance. If she ignores your request by interrupting or disrespecting you, you modify your own behavior and take the necessary actions to protect and restore your boundary. In this example, you'd simply stop sharing vulnerable information. This might mean that you shift the conversation to something less vulnerable, like the weather or the news. Or it might mean that you completely remove yourself from a conversation—leave the party, shut the door, walk away, hang up, or do whatever is needed to protect the boundary for yourself.

BUT ISN'T SOMETHING BETTER THAN NOTHING?

This is what I had always thought. I was so afraid to set boundaries because I was terrified that I'd end up with nothing. I had lived most of my life thinking that it was better to get just a little rather than nothing at all. I'd rather get a little attention than no attention. I'd rather get a tiny bit of money than no money. I'd rather have a warm body in the room than be alone. It was like I was perpetually starving and always settling for a few stale crumbs.

So let me tell you right now: something isn't necessarily better than nothing. When you're starving and settling for crumbs, you never, ever feel nourished or satisfied. When you settle for crumbs, you'll always be hungry, and you'll always feel desperate. This means that you must learn to say no to the crumbs. And let me tell you, when you're starving and desperate, this is really difficult to put into action.

But here's the deal. Whether or not you say no to the crumbs, you're going to end up hungry anyway. If you settle for a tiny bit of money, you'll still be broke. If you settle for just a warm body in the room, you'll still be lonely. If you settle for a little attention, you'll still feel desperately needy.

The only way out of this mess is to stop settling for less than you deserve. And yes, this might mean that you're hungry for a while. Or that you're lonely. Or that you're broke. But all those things were happening already, and when you stop accepting the stupid little stale bits of nothing, draw a line in the sand, and tell yourself that you are worth more than crappy crumbs, something amazing happens. You no longer feel desperate; you feel proud. You no longer feel needy; you feel strong. You no longer feel lonely; you feel patient. You no longer feel worthless; you feel worthy.

> The only way out of this mess is to stop settling for less than you deserve.

WHAT DO YOU EXPECT IN RETURN?

Similar to the spending and giving work, earning and receiving begins with you, your desires, your specific wants and needs. Rather than focus on what you hope to get or on how you'd like someone else to behave, the work starts with honoring your true self.

In the last chapter, I suggested listing twenty things that you were willing to spend and give your time, attention, and energy to. This chapter's work is the counterpart to that list. For each item listed, I'd like you to clearly define what you expect in return for your efforts. To build self-worth, you not only need to know where you want to give and spend your resources, you also need to have a healthy boundary for yourself about what you expect in return for your investment.

For example, do you want a loving relationship? If so, you not only need to be willing to spend and give your time, energy, and attention toward creating a loving relationship, you'd also need to require the same in return. This doesn't mean that you need to get back the same exact resource that you give. Maybe you give a lot of physical touch, and you get back a lot of listening. Maybe you give a lot of cooked meals, and you get back sweet sticky notes on the bathroom mirror. Remember, this isn't tit for tat. It's about being willing to give and willing to receive back what you rightfully deserve. This creates a relationship that is supportive and sustainable.

Or maybe you want a strong and healthy body. If so, you'd need to be willing to spend and give your time, energy, and attention toward doing what it takes to have a healthy body, and in return, you'd expect that your body would become stronger and more vibrant. If it doesn't, you'd need to change how you spend your energy. For instance, maybe you join a boot camp and work out like a madwoman, and instead of feeling stronger and more alive, you feel like you're a million years old and can barely lift yourself out of a chair. Instead of continuing to overspend yourself, you contain your efforts and wait. Much like a relationship, working with your body requires the same patience. Rather than trying to manipulate and enforce, you'll watch for feedback and work toward sustainability. Rather than depleting yourself, you'll move toward supporting yourself.

If you've been squeaking by on crumbs, it may be difficult for you to believe that you can actually receive enough to sustain and support you. So I suggest that you consciously give yourself permission to ask for what you need, require what you deserve, and expect fair compensation for what you give.

The mantras for earning and receiving are *I have permission to receive this. I have permission to earn this.*

> *Give yourself permission to ask for what you need.*

For example, you have permission to receive love. You have permission to receive attention. You have permission to receive kindness. You have permission to receive eye contact. You have permission to receive physical touch. You have permission to earn the money you deserve. You have permission to receive the relationship you deserve.

Reinforce your worthiness by refusing to settle for less than you deserve. Honor your true self, and respect that you deserve to earn and receive enough to sustain and protect yourself.

WORTHY WORK: WHERE YOU SLEEP

Take a picture of where you sleep exactly as it is in this moment. Don't wait for the day when your bed is perfectly made, and don't rush out to pick up brand-new Egyptian cotton five-hundred-thread-count sheets. Leave the stack of books on your bedside table exactly as it is, and leave last night's laundry lying right where it is on the floor. This isn't about recreating the Pottery Barn catalog. It's about taking an honest look at how you receive when it comes to resting.

As you know by now, I recommend using a photograph because you might miss the little details that you've become accustomed to. So whether you sleep in a plush bedroom of your own, on the couch in the den, or squished in between your five kids, two dogs, and seventeen cats, just take a quick snapshot of the scene.

When I'm looking at student photos, I'm not looking at whether or not their bedspread is pretty. I'm looking for how they honor the right to rest. I'm looking at the care and respect that goes into sleep. I'm looking for any clue that reinforces a sense of worthiness or worthlessness.

I'm not necessarily looking for blackout curtains or a certain number of throw pillows. I'm looking for how their sleeping space might reflect their capacity to receive kindness, gentleness, and affection. Worthiness means that you believe you are worth your own time and energy. And in this exercise, we're specifically looking at how you replenish and restore your time and energy. There is no right way to sleep, nor is there a perfect bedroom. This is more about noticing the unconscious ways that you settle for less than you deserve, where you might need to set a boundary around what you give away and expect in return, thereby reinforcing a sense of worthiness.

As in the other photos, my detective eye is searching for whether this person is reinforcing the idea that their true self is worth their time, attention, and energy or if they're ignoring or disregarding what the true self rightfully deserves.

To give you an idea of how this works, let me share a few examples.

REAL STORIES: ALEXA

Alexa, mother of three, signed up for class shortly after her divorce. As a corporate attorney, she felt confident and capable at work. Yet outside the office, she was timid and constantly second-guessed herself. She shared that her self-worth had taken a beating during the last few years of her marriage and that she constantly feels guilty for what her kids have gone through. She said, "When I have my kids, my extra time goes to them. When they're at their dad's, I work as much as possible. There's not a lot of 'me' time in my schedule—just work and kids." When Alexa posted her photo, I wasn't surprised to see a picture of the living room couch. There was one pillow and a throw blanket wadded up in the corner, a coffee table with a glass of water, some reading glasses, a stack of what looked like work papers, and at the foot of the couch were a few toys, a doll, some Legos, and a tractor.

I asked her to share what she saw in the photo. She said, "I see someone who doesn't even allow herself a bedroom. I gave our house to my ex, I continue to pay the mortgage for that house, I'm barely making ends meet, and I'm living in a crappy condo. I'm not even sleeping on a couch that I like. This apartment came furnished, and I'm just making do with what's there."

When asked if this photo showed a reinforcement of worthiness or a reinforcement of worthlessness, she said worthlessness. "My ex-husband has a bed and bedroom and a house. All three of my kids have their own bedrooms and beautiful little beds. And here I am sleeping on a couch. The embarrassing part is that the couch has a pull-out bed, but I won't even give myself that. I don't even remove the toys. I just sleep in a little ball in the corner."

When you look through the eyes of what she expects in return for what she gives, you can see a major discrepancy in compensation. Alexa overspent and under-received to the point that she had exhausted her money, her energy, and her well-being. To shift to the worthy cycle, she'd need to change at least one small thing to honor, respect, and care for her true self. Ideally, she wanted to find herself a four-bedroom apartment, but she had no extra money, time, or energy for a move. But building worthiness doesn't require a major shift, nor does it require money. Worthiness happens by changing your behavior just a little bit. In Alexa's case, she decided to use linens that she'd been storing in the hallway closet. She put sheets on the fold-out bed, allowed herself the generosity of two pillows, and brought out a cozy comforter. This didn't cost her a penny, yet it made a huge impact on her sense of worthiness. By giving herself a few extra moments at night where she removed the toys, pulled out the bed, and allowed herself a proper sleeping space, she reinforced that she has permission to receive rest, nurturing, and kindness.

She posted an after photo, with her bed made up—it looked cute and cozy. She wrote, "In my old house, in my old bedroom, I had this enormous and gorgeous bed. It looked like it was straight out of a catalog...the bedroom, the closet, the perfect everything. And I always hated sleeping in that room. And here is a picture of this tiny condo, with my nice little pull-out couch, and I couldn't be happier. Last night, I slept better than I have in years."

REAL STORIES: STEPHANIE

Stephanie, the owner of an organic bakery in the Pacific Northwest, shared that she needed help with her codependent tendencies. She shared that she felt responsible for her employees, friends, and her customers. She constantly worried about her extended family members and had a difficult time setting healthy boundaries. She said, "I don't know how to avoid taking on other people's problems. But I need a better way to live. I'm absolutely exhausted." The first thing that I noticed when I looked at Stephanie's photo was the magnificent bed in the center of the room. The headboard looked like it was made from old restored planks of wood, and the bedspread looked luxurious—although a tad dark and masculine. Her photo appeared to be quite picture perfect, but given what I knew about her, I had a hunch that this too may be showing her tendency to overgive and underearn.

When I asked her about her photo, she shared, "There's a lot about this photo that I actually love. I love my bed. I just bought it last year. I don't love the bedspread. It's more of my husband's taste rather than mine. When I'm looking for clues of where I don't receive enough in return, I see one thing that I can easily change. I love to read at night, yet I have no reading light and no books near my bed. My husband hates lights and complains when I read, so I just lie there in the dark until I finally fall asleep."

To move into the worthy cycle, she decided she needed to change a few things. First, she bought her husband an eye mask to block out light. She realized she didn't deserve to lie awake in the dark when there was a simple and kind remedy for both of them. Next, she gave herself a little nook for reading. She brought in a lamp from her guest bedroom and set it up on her nightstand with a stack of books and her reading glasses.

When she posted her after picture, she shared, "The lamp and the books make me so happy. It's like a little stack of gifts that I gave to myself. I used to dread going to sleep because I'd just spin out in my head in the dark and try to cope. Now, it's like I have a bunch of friends to hang out with. It's comforting and relaxing. Such an obvious thing, but I never saw it before."

By offering care for her true self, she reinforced the idea that she needed to protect what was rightfully hers. She deserved kindness and comfort. She deserved care and rest. And this didn't have to happen at her husband's expense. Instead, she found a way to care for him without settling for less than she deserved.

REAL STORIES: NICOLE

Nicole, an avid homesteader, signed up for my class to help her gain balance and confidence as a young mother. Most of her waking hours were spent child-rearing, working in her garden, or preserving what she had grown, while her husband tended to the livestock on their ranch. After trying to have children for years and after many heartbreaking miscarriages, they finally adopted a baby. A few months later, Nicole found out she was pregnant, and miraculously, she ended up having twins. In class, she shared that she never stops feeling grateful. She said, "Even though it's difficult to have three babies under three years old, it's worth every minute. I wouldn't change it for the world." In Nicole's picture, her bed was covered in toddlers and pets and books and blankets and pillows and stuffed animals. Every single inch of the bed was spoken for. It was a sweet scene depicting a very specific time in life—one where her children were little, where the family bed was not only the sleeping place but a safe space for the entire family.

She shared, "Having a family bed is important to me, and even though this looks like chaos, it's a sort of organized chaos that works for all of us. I'm not willing to sacrifice this experience right now. I know it's short-lived, and I'm okay with not getting a lot of sleep."

I admired her strength and her commitment to her vision. She was aware of her own responsibility in receiving rest and had made a conscious decision to sacrifice her quality of sleep during this time in motherhood. Yet I wanted to offer her a way not only to parent in the way she wanted but also to make sure that she received back what she deserved. I asked her if there was anything that she might change to reinforce a sense of her own worth. She didn't have any ideas.

I said, "Well, I only had one toddler, and in my experience, she seemed to have a knack for ending up sideways. For some reason, she always seemed to want to be pressing against my body while she slept. So I finally figured out that if I put a small pillow in between us, she would have something to press against, and I got to have uninterrupted sleep."

Nicole's eyes lit up. She said that she still had a long body pillow that she'd used for her pregnancy. Her bed had ample room to include the pillow so that she could carve out a little space for her own sleeping while still feeling connected to her kids and in alignment with her parenting style. Her after photo showed a bed that was similar to the first, yet there was now an additional long tube of a pillow. Comically, all three toddlers were lined up in a row, feet pressing into the pillow, sound asleep.

Nicole shared, "See all those feet against that pillow? That pillow used to be me! It's funny to see it in a photo and to realize that I didn't need to be sacrificing so much. I didn't even realize that there might be a way to give them what they need and also get a little more of what I need. I just bought a second body pillow so that my husband can do the same. An easy win."

Moving into the worthy cycle doesn't necessarily mean that you have to make grand and sweeping changes in your life. Rather, you change your behavior little by little. As you move into the worthy cycle by pulling out the sofa bed, placing a lamp and books on your bedside table, or carving out a little space for yourself, you start to gain momentum. The new behavior reinforces a sense of worthiness, making it easier and easier for you to set boundaries and ask for what you rightfully deserve.

YOUR WORTHY WORK

Very important: Under no circumstances are you allowed to do this exercise with the intention of self-shaming, adding to your to-do list, or causing yourself overwhelming shame spirals or anxiety. This exercise is only to be done with compassion and love.

Now it's your turn. Look at your picture with your detective eye. In the photo, do you see any evidence of what you require and what you receive? Do you see any evidence of where you're not receiving what you deserve? What do you notice? Do you see any evidence that may be reinforcing worthlessness?

You're looking for clues of where there's a disregard of care, respect, and support for your true self. This might look like a bedroom you don't love, sharing a bed with someone you don't like, or sleeping in an atmosphere that doesn't protect the sleep you rightfully deserve. You're also looking for clues of where you're overspending and giving away too much. You're looking at whether you see evidence that reinforces worthiness or reinforces worthlessness.

In the worthy cycle, you earn and receive in a way that reinforces that you are worth time, attention, and care. In this exercise, we are focusing on reinforcing worthiness by giving yourself permission to receive rest.

Take your photo and figure out a small change that will help you reinforce your own sense of worthiness. Find a way that you can deliberately receive more kindness, more care, and more rest. And then take action.

JOURNAL PROMPTS

1. Historically, where do you tend to under-receive or underearn? What type of consequences has this created in your life?
2. Where in your life do you need to ask for better compensation? What would be more fair? What request do you need to make? What boundary do you need to set?
3. Who do you know with strong boundaries? What is it like to have them in your life? What can you learn from them?
4. Who do you know with weak boundaries? What is it like to have them in your life? What can you learn from them?

CHAPTER 5
Chasing and Avoiding

It was Monday, which meant that once again, I was staring at a blank document and a blinking cursor. I have a rhythm when I'm writing a book, and every Monday morning begins a new cycle where I dump all my thoughts onto the new chapter's blank page and start to form an outline for what I need to write in the upcoming week. The remaining weekdays are spent filling in the pages, editing, and rewriting, so that by Friday, I have a rough draft. Over the weekend, I rest my brain and come up with new ideas so that by the following Monday morning, I'm ready to start over with a blank page again.

Typically, my Mondays start before the rest of the house wakes up. Quietly, I shuffle out to the kitchen to make some coffee. I see my messy hair and my ratty blue cashmere sweater reflected back to me from the window over the sink. Beyond my reflection, I see only black night. I wake early because I've made a deal with the writing muse: I show up to do the work, and in exchange, I expect to receive a fresh batch of ideas. This contract has worked for years, and I expect her to uphold her side of the bargain. By the end of the first cup of coffee, I usually have a queue of ideas ready to spill forth onto the blank pages that wait for me. I'll start rehearsing ideas in my mind, I'll make little notes in my Moleskine journal, and once I'm adequately caffeinated, I'll begin to type the words, empty out my brain, and start the process of my work week.

Today, however, for no apparent reason other than a strange gift from the universe, I slept in. I didn't even know my body had the ability to sleep past sunrise anymore. Disoriented, grateful, and possibly still dreaming, I walked to the kitchen and poured myself a cup of already-made coffee. The world was brightly lit beyond the kitchen window, and the hummingbirds were already zipping back and forth between the bougainvillea and the hydrangea in the courtyard. Blank white pages loomed in my head, and yet no words appeared. I drank the first cup, and then another, trying to get the brain engine to start chugging. But nothing came.

A hint of desperation, fear, or maybe even dread started to make its way into the periphery of my consciousness. Like a thin gray smoke slipping under the door, through the open windows, and down the chimney. Subtle enough to not be noticed, and now, only in hindsight, do I realize how frightening the unrecognized threat of doom had been. My muse had failed to show. Rather than a spark of insight, I only found reams of blank white paper occupying my thoughts.

Mindlessly, I started cleaning the house. I collected the weekend's accumulation of beach towels, and I gathered up the forgotten piles of Sunday *Times* from yesterday's sunny afternoon reading. I walked through each room, picking up a smattering of laundry left on floors. I watered the plants. I found at least eighty-five different water cups cluttering up every horizontal surface. I took drumsticks out of the freezer to thaw for dinner.

The ghosts of empty pages continued to haunt my thoughts—not overtly, mind you. By this point, I was more focused on the little housekeeping tasks that occupied my attention. The toothbrush caddy that needed to be wiped dry. The bathroom trash that needed to be emptied. The painting in the hallway that needed to be straightened. My sock drawer was pure chaos, and the immediate organization of all socks suddenly became a matter of life and death.

Without direction and without purpose, I puttered around for most of the morning. All the while, a hazy feeling of gloom was gaining on me. A low hum of anxiety, barely audible in the distance, seemed to be coming for me, like a runaway train gaining speed, vibrating off the rails in my direction. A brief image of empty white pages scattered across the surface of my mind. I tried not to notice.

The blinking cursor can wait, I told myself. *I need to take a shower first. I always write better when my hair is clean.* For the record, this isn't true. I've written plenty of words with dirty hair. But I stepped into the shower and turned on the water.

While freezing water pelted my legs, I waited for it to warm up. And I waited. And waited. For several minutes, I waited for any sign of warmth. But it still ran ice cold.

Still in my towel, I took a quick trip to the water heater only to find an error code blinking on its screen. I hoped for an easy fix, so I sat down (still in my towel) and Googled the error code, hoping to find a do-it-yourself video on YouTube. This filled me with an almost noticeable sense of relief. In the moment, I didn't register the relief; I simply became absorbed in researching fix-it videos. In the recesses of my mind, I kinda sorta remembered that I was supposed to be doing something important this morning, but that wasn't even a fully formed memory. I didn't realize that the anxiety that had colored the background of my morning now came down to a singular purpose: fix the water heater. The looming doom faded into the background as I got dressed, found the toolbox, watched fix-it videos, and made calls to plumbers.

Several hours passed before I realized the humor and the irony of what I'd been doing. I'd spent half a day avoiding writing a chapter on avoiding.

And this is always the way it goes with avoiding. At best, you catch it after the fact. Most of the time, you don't even realize that you're doing it. And this is what makes it so difficult to spot, let alone change. At best, you'll see it when you end up with an overly organized sock drawer rather than a written chapter. But most of the time, avoidance is much more corrosive and difficult to recognize and goes on a lot longer than half a day.

THE USEFUL DISTRACTION

In this chapter, we are looking at the behaviors of chasing and avoiding—behaviors that unconsciously distract you from uncomfortable emotions. These are behaviors that help you cope, numb, avoid, repress, or ignore your feelings. This can look like eating your way through a big bag of chips, binge-watching Netflix, drinking, smoking, shopping, or getting lost in the colorful world of your smartphone—something that distracts you and offers a hit of short-term gratification rather than long-term satisfaction. Chasing and avoiding can even look like something beneficial—going for a run, rushing cupcakes to your daughter's third-grade classroom, or madly organizing your sock drawer. The behavior itself can take almost any form, but the root cause of the behavior—denial and repression of emotion—keeps you stuck in the worthless cycle. To build self-worth, you have to honor your true self, and you can't do that if you're ignoring, repressing, numbing, or checking out from your emotions.

Chasing and avoiding are two sides of the same coin. Chasing is the unconscious attempt to get to a better feeling, while avoiding is the unconscious attempt to get away from a bad feeling. Some people resonate with one word more than the other, and others use the words interchangeably. Regardless of whether you identify more with the idea of chasing a good feeling or avoiding a bad feeling, the root problem is the same—an incapacity to experience discomfort, specifically an uncomfortable, naturally occurring emotion.

Bringing to light any habit of chasing and avoiding is critical for worthy work. Since these behaviors are typically

> *Chasing is the unconscious attempt to get to a better feeling, while avoiding is the unconscious attempt to get away from a bad feeling.*

unconscious, trying to bring your attention to them to permanently change your habits can be quite difficult. Yet when you're chasing and avoiding and you lack emotional awareness, you stay stuck in a cycle that only reinforces worthlessness. To build self-worth, you need to be able to discern what emotion you're feeling in real time, and you need to be able to take action based on the wisdom embedded within an emotion. So in this chapter, I want to give you a little more understanding about the emotions (conscious or unconscious) that may be keeping you stuck in the worthless cycle.

Although emotional pain is uncomfortable, it arises for an important reason and offers you crucial feedback about your life. When you deny your emotions by chasing and avoiding, you miss valuable guidance from your true self. This could look like a pushing away, disregarding, or compartmentalizing of emotion. This could look like not wanting to cry during a fight, so you suck in your sadness and muscle yourself through the conversation without allowing yourself to feel the sadness and loss. This could look like skirting around a difficult conversation by avoiding phone calls and texts, hoping it will all go away. This could look like trying to conceal weakness, so you cough or clear your throat rather than allow your voice to betray your sense of vulnerability.

Disregarding your feelings might also show up as distraction or self-soothing. It could be as small as picking up your phone when you feel bored. It could be madly cleaning your house to avoid a feeling of powerlessness. It could be bingeing on Netflix to avoid a feeling of loneliness. Instead of ignoring or burying the feeling, you run away from your feelings and throw yourself into anything that brings a little relief.

When you distract yourself from your emotions, worthlessness is unconsciously running the show. This is what happens when you push pause and have a margarita. This is what happens when you put your feelings into a box while you go for a run. This is what happens when you file away your feelings for a rainy day while keeping busy at the office.

The problem with this is that the more you run from your feelings, the more there are to run from. The more you avoid, the more there is to avoid. Emotions don't disappear when you ignore them; they merely fester and wreak havoc behind the scenes. When you avoid a feeling, you're merely procrastinating. The feeling will wait. And while it waits, it will get bigger, uglier, more complicated, and more confusing.

As the pain and discomfort increase, the intensity of the avoidance tactic must also increase. The greater the pain, the more intensity you need to distract yourself from it. What

> *The more you run from your feelings, the more there are to run from.*

starts off as a seemingly benign habit can grow into a life-shattering addiction. Whether you are drinking, eating, starving, spending, gambling, snorting, sniffing, smoking, running, or anything-else-ing, when you continue a behavior despite the negative consequences that it creates in your life, it means—at its root—that you're in pain.

Show me someone who can't stop punishing themselves, someone who can't stop underearning and under-receiving, someone who can't stop overspending or overgiving, someone who can't put their phone, drink, or laptop down, someone who can't just be here in this moment without having to alter it or self-soothe through it, and I'll show you someone who doesn't know how to handle their heart: the intangible center from which all emotions flow. I'll show you someone who has made a habit of chasing and avoiding. It's a painful cycle that can only be ended one way: learning how to open your heart.

A STRONG BACKBONE AND AN OPEN HEART

When I speak about the heart, I'm not referring to the tangible muscular organ that pumps blood through your body; I'm talking about the intangible gateway to the elusive inner world of emotions. This intangible heart is the portal to emotion, the epicenter of where emotions are felt, but it's also the birthplace or the spring from which they flow. Through understanding the messages embedded in your emotions, you deepen your connection to your true self.

Emotions are kind of like colors. When I talk about emotion, I am referring to a reaction, conscious or unconscious, a phenomenon or physiological response that plays out in the theater of your body, a response that colors the way you experience life itself. In the world of colors, there are primary colors—red, yellow, and blue—and you can mix these colors together to make any other color imaginable. Emotions are similar. There's a basic group of them, and then, depending on how they're mixed together, you will experience countless variations and intensities of emotion throughout a single day or even a single hour. There are a few common emotions that almost every human feels (or tries not to feel) some of the time. These emotions evolved to offer specific guidance—a map that many of us, unfortunately, lost long ago when we forgot how to tap into how we really feel. So even though there is a full spectrum of other feelings—beautiful, terrible, exquisite, and sublime as they are—I'm going to teach what I've found to be the four core worthy emotions.

THE FOUR CORE EMOTIONS

Each of the four core emotions evolved with a distinct and clear function, and you can use their wisdom to build self-worth.

These four core emotions are also quite uncomfortable and are the main culprits for chasing and avoiding. When these emotions are misunderstood, repressed, ignored, or avoided, they can lead you straight down a rabbit hole of worthlessness. Yet when you expand your capacity to experience them, you'll be able to gain crucial feedback that will keep you in the worthy cycle.

The first of these emotions is fear. The second is what I call shame-guilt; this isn't really a word, but for worthy work, shame and guilt tend to go hand in hand. The third core emotion is anger. The fourth core emotion is sadness.

I like to think of worthiness as two things: an open heart and a strong backbone. This can be a physical way that you hold yourself. Think standing tall, shoulders back, chest open like Wonder Woman or Superman. Taking a superhero posture is a physical way to practice and embody worthiness. Beyond the physical expression, having an open heart and strong backbone is also a metaphorical way to hold yourself that requires both strength and flexibility. A strong backbone means that you're ready to take action to protect and care for your true self. A strong backbone helps you set boundaries, encourages you to ask for what you deserve, and keeps you from overspending your resources. An open heart offers you the flexibility to experience a full range of emotion, providing you crucial real-time feedback from your true self.

But what does it mean to open your heart?

I live just a few blocks from a gorgeous white-sand beach. Just around the south point of the beach, the sand ends and black bones of eroded rocks jut out into the ocean. At low tide, you can walk out on those rocks and see all kinds of creatures: mussels, coral, hermit crabs, starfish. One of the most beautiful creatures in the tide pool is the sea anemone. It looks like an underwater flower—sometimes pink, sometimes blue, sometimes purple, with hundreds of tiny tentacle petals swaying back and forth in the small pools of water left behind by the tide. When left alone, they are open and relaxed, and their tentacles collect nourishment that comes in with the water.

When I was a kid, my cousin showed me a trick. She touched her finger into the center of a sea anemone, and the tentacles immediately closed up into a small round ball. What once looked like an underwater flower now looked like a tight green bud.

When you can't handle your feelings, your intangible heart closes, similar to a sea anemone. When it's open and relaxed, it's available to sort through the information flowing through your life. And when it closes up, it's not able to process information, receive nourishment, or offer you necessary feedback. So the work is to keep your heart open, even if it gets poked.

When I talk about keeping your heart open, I'm asking you to stop yourself from turning away from your emotional center. I'm talking about staying open even when you feel discomfort. I'm talking about allowing your feelings to run their natural course so that you can receive the crucial feedback and life-giving information that they offer.

You can think of your heart like a sea anemone or like a flower that remains open to the sun. You can think of it like a valve that's open so information can naturally flow through it. Choose any image that helps you. The goal of worthy work is to keep the heart open and relaxed so that you can process your feelings and stay consciously connected to your true self.

My Monday morning story may simply look like a matter of procrastination, and it was, but I wasn't necessarily procrastinating to avoid my work. I was avoiding a feeling. Actually, I was avoiding a bunch of uncomfortable feelings.

I didn't deliberately check in with my emotions. I didn't face them head-on. Nor did I open my heart to the pain that echoed in the background. Instead, I unconsciously distracted myself from the doomy-gloomy mixture of feelings that rumbled in the periphery. Without really giving it a conscious thought, I had a vague sense of knowing that there was pain under the surface, but I didn't want to deal with it. This distraction (whether you call it avoiding or chasing) is a coping mechanism, but there's a major flaw in this strategy, because there is no way to keep pain at bay forever.

To pull myself out of my unconscious avoidance spinout, I had to do three things. First, I had to open my heart; this means that I needed to deliberately turn toward my inner emotional landscape. Second, I needed to check in with each of the four core worthy emotions. Third, I needed to take action based on the wisdom of each emotion.

To stay connected to your true self and consciously open your heart, you'll need to become aware of your feelings, become conscious of any habits you use to avoid your feelings, and learn to trust your heart for guidance. Although certain emotions might be more dominant, they do not stand alone. In every situation, you should consider each of the core worthy emotions: fear, shame-guilt, anger, and sadness. Even if you're not consciously aware of these feelings, you may find that one, several, or all of the emotions are present, even when they aren't noticeable on the surface.

> " To stay connected to your true self and consciously open your heart, you'll need to become aware of your feelings, become conscious of any habits you use to avoid your feelings, and learn to trust your heart for guidance. "

FEAR

For most people, fear is so pervasive that it's almost impossible to think about what life might be like without it. The beige, low-grade stress in the background of your day? Fear. The anxiety that keeps your head spinning at night? Fear. That worry about missing out, not keeping up, falling behind, or that you're never going to find your life's true purpose? Fear. In all its intensities, from worry to terror, fear plays an important role in your life.

Fear is intensely uncomfortable, but it holds information that's imperative for building self-worth. Fear wants you to pay attention. It wants to prevent you from anything that threatens your well-being. It evolved to keep you alive and to keep your resources intact. Fear is an appropriate response to a lack of resources—food, shelter, safety, energy, health. When you're avoiding fear, you're cut off from its wisdom and will miss messages that point you to safety.

In your body, fear feels fast, anxious, nervous, worried. It's a hum, a vibration. This is the signal to get clear on what's being threatened. Rather than avoid this feeling, you can appreciate the intention: to keep you and your resources safe.

When you don't honor fear, you'll easily and often unconsciously deplete your resources through overspending and underearning. You can see this in my Gucci dress example. I wasn't aware of the natural fear that wanted to keep me safe from overspending my money. If I had been aware, I would have felt worry or anxiety about spending money that would create a dangerous financial situation. In hindsight, I can see how deeply fear colored that entire day—fear of not being enough, fear of not keeping up, fear of missing out, fear of being found to be a fraud. Yet rather than acknowledging the fear or being conscious of the fear, I compulsively spent money—a classic example of chasing and avoiding.

SHAME-GUILT

Much has been said about the difference between shame and guilt. For the purposes of this work, I'm going to group shame and guilt together (calling it shame-guilt), because their functions are similar: basically to keep you from getting way off course in human relationships.

Guilt is a reaction to *doing something* wrong or bad, and shame is the feeling of *being or having* innate qualities that are wrong or bad. Shame comes up when you feel that you *are* something bad, wrong, not enough. But these two feelings feed off each other, because you can start to tell yourself that you did something bad because you are a bad person who does wrong things because you are wrong... You get the picture?

People often misunderstand shame-guilt, thinking that this is the feeling of worthlessness. However, when you allow yourself to experience the natural course of the emotions, shame and guilt offer valuable feedback that will help guide you back into the worthy cycle. Shame and guilt evolved to help forge social bonds. When you repress this information, you'll fail to hear the important message embedded in this emotion. Shame and guilt want you to repair a lost connection; however, an unconscious distraction takes you in the opposite direction. Shame and guilt want you to reach out, connect, and repair your social bonds. The distracted state keeps you isolated, lonely, and disconnected—reactions that keep you stuck in the worthless cycle. When you honor shame and guilt, you take action to repair bonds, you honor your need for connection, and you show respect to your true self.

In your body, shame-guilt feels like a pit in your stomach; it's a slow, painful sensation and often feels like you're being torn or punched in the gut or like you're burning on fire.

When shame-guilt unconsciously fuels your behavior, you can end up doing the exact opposite action of what it wants. Rather than connect, you disconnect. This puts you into a spiral of avoiding and chasing that gains momentum and erodes your self-worth.

ANGER

Stand in line at the post office, the grocery store checkout, or the slowest moving line anywhere—the DMV—and you might get to the point where you're rolling your eyes, sighing, tapping your toes, leaning on one hip and then the other, checking the clock, sighing again—basic signs of impatience. You know that growing feeling of frustration that you get when someone or something is in your way? That's anger. At home, when your spouse forgets to pick up toilet paper and you really don't want to have to go out again tonight and *Ugh, why do I have to do everything around here?* That's anger too. Coming out of Target, when you just don't have time to add anything else to your plate and up walks some well-meaning, dolphin-loving, clipboard-holding survey taker and you hold up your hand as you walk by and just try to get out of the parking lot without having to get involved in saving any part of the planet? You guessed it—anger.

Out of the four emotions, I think anger is the most critical when it comes to cultivating worthiness because anger is the signal of unfairness and a boundary violation. To contain your overgiving and stand up for what you deserve to receive, you'll need access to anger's wisdom. When anger is repressed or denied, your boundaries deteriorate, which eventually leads to a complete and utter loss of self. Anger is the appropriate response to unfair compensation and underearning, and its message is critical for protecting what's rightfully yours. If you don't take the action needed when anger first presents itself, the ignored anger will often fester to hatred, fury, or rage to get your attention. Anger wants you to protect your valuable resources.

In your body, anger feels fast, strong, and hot, like a surge of wanting to fight, protect, and defend.

When you don't honor anger, you'll end up in a double-bagging situation like I did. Rather than acknowledging the appropriate response to unfair compensation, I pushed it down and focused on how I could appear more likable. If I had been in touch with my anger, I would have felt just a tinge of annoyance. The reasonable and natural response wouldn't have been full-blown rage, violence, or any kind of reactive outburst. It would have simply been a little heat within me to help empower me to ask for what was fair.

SADNESS

From feeling slightly bummed or having a bit of the blues to being hurt or having intense emotions of sorrow, despair, heartbreak, or grief, sadness comes in many forms and a variety of intensities. When you're home for the eighty-fifth Friday night alone, eating pizza in your pajamas while the rest of the world seems to be out having a great time, making friends, falling in love, getting married, and having babies without you? That lonely, achy, outcast-y feeling? Sadness. When you really thought someone liked you and you find out that they don't, at least not in *that* way? That heartbreaking, chest-pain, despairing, hopeless feeling? Sadness. When your mom died decades ago and you're in the vitamin aisle minding your own business until some woman passes you with your mom's signature perfume wafting behind her, and for one tiny moment, it's like you just lost your mom all over again? That tidal wave of grief-stricken bereavement that thwacks you across your gut and buckles your knees? Sadness.

Sadness is the feeling that comes up when you lose something of value. The pain is caused by clinging to something that is already gone. Sadness evolved to help you cope with letting go. Loss is supposed to be painful. Otherwise, we wouldn't try so hard to keep our loved ones safe, our social bonds healthy, and our support systems intact. Loss is tragic; it means that you have invested in something that you no longer have.

Sadness is an invitation to receive. It wants you to seek comfort, caretaking, and help. Sadness is a natural response to loss, and it wants you to spend less and receive more to replenish your resources. When you repress and deny sadness, you lose valuable information that tells you to slow down, rejuvenate, and recover.

In your body, sadness feels slow and heavy. It literally makes the physical space around your heart hurt.

If you look at my life right around the time of the double-bagging incident, I could easily make a case that I was repressing all four worthy emotions, and that to distract myself from this overwhelming pain, I engaged in a debilitating degree of chasing and avoiding. But as an example, let's just focus on how this played out in distracting me from sadness. The truth is that there were several painful losses during that time, the most acute being the loss of my yoga retreat center. This was a dream that I'd had for years and one in which I'd invested so much time, money, blood, sweat, and tears. Rather than acknowledging how devastating this failure had been and how sad I was to walk away from my dream, I just kept chasing and avoiding. If I'd been in touch with my sadness, I would have understood that I needed to rest, grieve, restore, and let go. Rather than doing what was needed to replenish my resources, I unconsciously avoided sadness by overspending and underearning until I reached a financial, emotional, and physical breaking point.

STOP DISTRACTING AND START FEELING

Let's revisit my Monday morning procrastination adventure. Like I said, it's difficult to spot the chasing and avoiding when it's happening because it serves a function: to unconsciously conceal an uncomfortable emotion. So the work is to remind yourself to check in with all four core emotions often. This is the first line of defense when you've drifted off track, have a habit you're trying to break, or can't seem to get out of the worthless cycle.

When I do an honest check-in with myself, more often than not, I can source all four worthy emotions. Therefore, instead of just checking in with the dominant emotion, I want you to get into the habit of assuming that all four are present.

First, look for anything in the fear family—the emotional response to danger. Fear encompasses worry, anxiety, panic, terror, and everything in between. Ask yourself *What am I afraid of?* And then be as specific as possible. Fear wants you to remain alert so that you can stay away from threats. It wants to keep you safe. The work here is to get specific about a conscious action (rather than a chasing/avoiding reaction) that will help to alleviate the fear.

Tracing back through my Monday morning, I can definitely find fear. I was afraid of being a failure, afraid of being a slacker, afraid of not being good enough. I was afraid of all kinds of things, but the biggest fear was really quite simple: I was afraid to sit down in front of the empty page. To get myself back in the worthy cycle, I had to be able to honor the fear instead of unconsciously reacting to it. That meant I had to sit down, feel the fear, and keep typing anyway.

Next, check in with the shame-guilt family—the emotional response to possible social disconnection. This encompasses embarrassment, self-consciousness, all the way to rejection and ostracism. Ask yourself *What am I ashamed of?* And then be as specific as possible. Shame wants you to connect, share, and engage with your community. The work here is to get specific about a conscious action (rather than a chasing/avoiding reaction) that helps move you toward connection.

I can absolutely find some shame-guilt going on behind the scenes on Monday morning. Rather than sitting down to that scary blank page, rather than being vulnerable and willing to do even a shoddy job at connecting with you, I disconnected and got caught up with fix-it-yourself YouTube videos. To get myself back in the worthy cycle, I had to be willing to share my true self, which is why I chose to share my procrastination story here. Rather than stay aloof and disconnected, the way to worthiness required humility and honesty.

Next, check in with the anger family—the emotional response to boundary violation and unfairness. This encompasses irritation, annoyance, and aggravation and can go all the way to fury, rage, and seething contempt. Ask yourself *What am I angry about?* And then be as specific as possible. Anger wants you to protect your resources, honor your boundaries, and receive what you deserve. The work here is to get specific about a conscious action (rather than a chasing/avoiding reaction) that will restore your boundaries and protect your resources.

Now this feeling was a little bit more difficult for me to find on Monday. No one had overtly wronged me; in fact, this scenario didn't involve anyone other than me. But when I asked myself what I was angry about, oddly and embarrassingly, I was just kind of mad at the universe. I was angry that I didn't have ideas that morning. I was annoyed that the muse didn't deliver. I felt like being a writer was simply too hard. It felt unfair. To get myself back into the worthy cycle, I had to channel that anger into protecting my boundaries. Rather than allow myself to squander away hours, days, and even years, I had to contain my compulsive avoiding and procrastination and force myself to just put my butt in the chair. The laundry would wait. The sock drawer would survive. A plumber would fix the water heater. But if I really wanted the words to be written, it would be up to me and me alone.

Lastly, check in with the sadness family—the emotional response to loss. This can encompass a feeling of disappointment or hurt and go from melancholy all the way to despair and grief. Ask yourself *What am I sad about?* And then be as specific as possible. Sadness wants you to retreat and rest so that you can restore and rejuvenate. The work here is to get specific about a conscious action (rather than a chasing/avoiding reaction) that will help you replenish your resources.

When I checked with sadness, I could feel the closed-up sea anemone bud within me. It took a few minutes of compassionate presence to gain the courage to face what lay hidden. I had to relax, breathe, and then metaphorically turn my attention toward the source of pain. Tears flowed as I found a deep well of loss within me. And this had nothing to do with book writing, nor did it have anything to do with the failure of a muse to uphold her end of the bargain. In fact, the sadness was not even noticeable on the surface of my Monday, yet it was probably the greatest source of pain that I was avoiding. Hence, this unrecognized grief was probably the dominant influence in my listlessness, my avoidance, and my procrastination on Monday, and I wouldn't have found it without deliberate and careful consideration.

The truth is that this is my daughter's senior year of high school, the last year that she will be asleep in bed while I work through the morning. It's the last year of this particular season of motherhood for me. And this loss cuts sharply and painfully behind the scenes of my days. It's a necessary and beautiful pain, a tribute to the fact that something that I have loved deeply is coming to an end. And although I know that I will be entering a new season of life and motherhood, there is a palpable sadness and grief to attend to. To move into the worthy cycle, I needed to acknowledge this poignant heartbreak—privately, to my own self. I needed to recognize that I am hurting and I need care and attention. I need to honor and respect myself and be careful with myself as I move through this season. This doesn't mean that I stop writing, teaching, cleaning, cooking, or paying the bills. Rather it means that I need to be aware that there's an extra tax on my resources right now and that I need to be more generous with myself.

Notice that my most profound pain had no overt relationship to worthiness or worthlessness. Yet by distracting myself from this sadness, I inadvertently took actions that reinforced a sense of worthlessness. The chasing and avoiding cost me a day of writing. The procrastinating deteriorated my sense of self-worth. I felt like I had been taken hostage by the worthless cycle. And the cause of all of it was an unwillingness to acknowledge the deep well of sadness within me.

Any time you find that you're unable to escape the

worthless cycle, I suggest checking for unconscious chasing and avoiding. Give consideration and thought to all four worthy emotions, and deliberately take action based on the emotional feedback. Fear wants you to keep your resources safe. Shame-guilt wants you to repair and renew social bonds. Anger wants you to fight for what you deserve. And sadness wants you to let go and restore your reserves. By taking just a few moments for contemplation, you'll put an end to any unconscious distraction and move yourself back into a place of building self-worth.

THE WISDOM OF EMOTIONS

In class, I give my students an assignment to help them become more aware of chasing and avoiding. I ask them to observe themselves for one day and to take note of any habits, distractions, compulsive actions, or the desire to check out. From the space of a compassionate witness, I ask them to notice how they work, rest, eat, drink, watch TV, use their phone, use social media, call a friend, et cetera. This is to help them figure out how they typically distract themselves and for how long the distraction lasts. Rather than sleepwalking around the worthless cycle, this helps them bring awareness to triggers and unconscious reactions.

For example, you might find that your compulsive Amazon Prime habit gets hot and heavy late in the evening after your kids are sound asleep. Rather than face your husband's seemingly insatiable sex drive and your own fear, guilt, anger, and sadness about the state of your marriage, you scroll through endless things that you do not want or need. You chase the next little dopamine fix, hit the *Buy Now* button, and avoid the mess of your life.

Or maybe you find that you've been absentmindedly gobbling handfuls of trail mix, and by bringing awareness to this habit, you realize that every time your mother calls, you head to the pantry. Instead of allowing yourself to acknowledge how much discomfort these calls have created, you've been pushing away the feelings and popping another handful of peanuts and raisins into your mouth.

Or maybe you find that every single time you go out to dinner with your friends, you compulsively offer to pay for everyone's meal. And once you realize that you're doing this, you become even more alarmed because you can't seem to stop yourself from doing it. When you check in with the core emotions and find a cocktail of repressed feelings—shame-guilt, fear, sadness, anger—you might realize that you've been overcompensating and chasing an ideal image rather than being honest and vulnerable.

Changing habits and bringing awareness to unconscious behavior is difficult. It takes practice and patience. Your work here isn't to find fault or berate yourself for anything. Rather, the work is to get to know yourself and check in with what's really going on under the surface so that you can offer more attention, care, and respect to your true self. Little by little, you'll find it easier to dip under the surface of distraction, feel the quality of true emotion driving any distracted behavior, and then quickly move yourself back into the worthy cycle.

As practice, I'd love for you to do this exercise yourself. Set a timer so that you remember to check in at least five times in your day—ideally, you want to have at least one check-in for every part of your typical day. Break your day into segments: for example, morning before school drop-off, commute, work time, after school to dinner, after dinner, after kids go to bed. For each of the segments, use your detective eye to observe your behavior. Notice if you're engaged in anything that may serve the purpose of distracting, numbing, avoiding, or chasing. Without any judgment, simply write down the behavior and the general time that it occurs.

Once you've finished logging one entire day, go back through any distracting, avoiding, chasing, numbing segments and dig a little deeper. This type of contemplation takes focus, generosity, and a willingness to open that interior sea anemone of a heart. You'll need to gently turn inward toward hidden pain and be willing to hear feedback from your true self. This isn't easy, and the information can be quite elusive. No matter what you find, this turning inward and focusing on your true self will always reinforce the idea that you are worth your own time, kindness, and attention. By keeping your heart open and your backbone strong and living as if your feelings deserve your time, attention, and respect, you always reinforce worthiness.

WORTHY WORK: SCREEN TIME

This chapter is about examining unconscious behavior, so instead of taking a picture of a scene in your home, I want you

> *By keeping your heart open and your backbone strong and living as if your feelings deserve your time, attention, and respect, you always reinforce worthiness.*

to figure out how to analyze your average screen time. Choose the screen that you use the most often—smartphone or tablet—and then take a screenshot of your usage. Don't wait for the day that you accidentally left your phone at home, and don't wait for the day when you've white-knuckled yourself through an afternoon without Instagram. There is no good or bad information here—it's only feedback. I want you to see an honest accounting of how often you use your device and how much time you're spending. This is about becoming aware of habitual distraction and waking up if you're mindlessly drifting off into the worthless cycle.

In this exercise, it's important to take a photo, because opening the screen settings app can easily end up leading you right back into the vortex of mindlessness. The work here is to stay focused on the information within the photo rather than clicking on apps or trying to change device settings. So whether you see fourteen hours of TikTok and the remaining ten on Facebook, or whether you see five hours of the Stocks app and two hours of news, or whether all your time has been spent on the phone to your mother, just take a quick snapshot of the screen.

When I'm looking at student photos, I'm not only looking for the amount of time they spend or what app they happen to use the most. I'm looking for clues of where there's a disregard of care, respect, and support for true self. This might look like spending time (key word: *spend*) on an app that doesn't give much—or anything—in return, an unexpected amount of time that can't really be accounted for, or where they may unconsciously be avoiding uncomfortable emotions. I'm looking for any clue that reinforces a sense of worthiness or worthlessness.

As in the other photos, my detective eye is searching for whether this person is reinforcing the idea that their true self is worth their time, attention, and energy or if they're ignoring or disregarding what the true self rightfully deserves.

To give you an idea of how this works, let me share a few examples.

REAL STORIES: KELLY

Kelly, a jewelry designer and owner of an upscale Hollywood boutique, joined my class to help her find a way to bring more balance into her life. She grew up on the East Coast, and after college, she moved to California and began making handmade jewelry. After a decade of having a small and devoted clientele, a few celebrities found her work and began wearing her pieces. Her business exploded overnight. She shared, "I live, breathe, and sleep my work now. I've worked my whole life to get to this place, and I don't want to blow it." Yet as her business became more successful, her personal life suffered. She said, "I'm so afraid that I'm going to end up alone, but at this point, it's all about work. There's no time for a relationship. I can't even make time to see my friends!"

Kelly was astonished when she took a close look at her average screen time. She had thought she was using her phone to "unwind" at night. She said, "If you were to ask me about my phone use, I would have said that I spend about fifteen minutes on Instagram. I can't believe that I'm spending hours per night scrolling mindlessly."

When I asked her why she opened Instagram in the first place, she said, "I think I open it because I feel lonely and bored. So I start scrolling. I'm always hoping that the next picture, the next person, or the next post might be something fun or something that makes me feel good. Or sometimes I open it to check to see who liked my post or who commented. It's like I'm looking to be affirmed or looking to belong, so I scroll hoping that I'll feel connected to people I care about, but in the end, I typically just feel bad about myself. It seems like everyone else is out there living a life, and I'm just over here eating cold pizza in my pajamas, pretending to belong."

Beneath Kelly's phone use was a sincere desire for connection and community. Yet instead of investing in real relationships, she distracted herself from loneliness by mindlessly scrolling. By avoiding loneliness and boredom and chasing artificial connection, she put herself smack-dab in the middle of the worthless cycle on a nightly basis. The first step was to break her habit: either delete the app or find something to take its place. Just having to search for the app, reload it, or login again helps to interrupt the mindlessness and bring attention to what she was choosing in that moment.

She said, "Once I saw that I was spending ten hours a week on something that made me feel terrible and ended up with me feeling even more lonely, I decided to bank those hours for guilt-free hang out time with my friends." For the past year, she had been telling herself that she was too busy to go to parties, meet up for coffee, or join a girls' getaway with her friends. Now she knew the truth; where she once mindlessly spent hours per day, she would now consciously spend time and energy caring for the relationships she valued most.

"I've also decided that if I'm bored or lonely, I'll text a friend before logging into Instagram. Maybe I'll even FaceTime them and we can eat cold pizza together." She laughed. "I think I need to acknowledge the loneliness rather than try to numb it out."

REAL STORIES: TAMMY

Tammy, a hospital administrator, had a strong work ethic and was devoted to her church. She shared, "I was raised with southern values. I work hard. I love my family, and I do what I can for my community." She still lived in the neighborhood where she was born and raised. She signed up for class to help her mend her broken heart after a breakup. She said, "I thought he was the one. We were both raised here, and everyone knew us as a couple. I don't know how to start over. I feel like I missed my chance. Everyone else is married and having kids. I don't know what I did wrong."

Tammy was shocked to see how much time she spent on dating apps, and she was too embarrassed to share her picture in class. She said, "I am on my phone all day long, before work, at work, after work. I log in here and there. It feels like I'm on the app for only a few minutes a day, but numbers don't lie. I'm on the apps way more than I thought. I'm mortified."

When I asked Tammy what prompted her to pick up her phone and open an app, she said she usually gets a notification. "I can't hear the sound without needing to go pick up my phone and see what it is. I get butterflies in my stomach just thinking about it. It's exciting to think that the guy might be the one. As soon as I hear the ding, I can't concentrate. I have to know who it is." But after the initial hit of excitement, she said she typically felt hollow, nervous, and uneasy. She said, "I pick up my phone thinking that it's going to be the one. But then the guy is usually a flake or ghosts me or just wants to hook up. I end up feeling rejected and stupid."

Even though Tammy sincerely wanted to find a partner, her automatic response to the notifications kept her mindlessly using the apps and stuck in the worthless cycle. Rather than mending her broken heart, she unconsciously put her heart at risk several times a day. The app played into her vulnerability of wanting to find the one yet never satisfied her true desire: to be cared for. Bringing awareness and attention to this part of her life helped to bring light to the larger problem of unconscious distraction.

Many of today's apps are designed for the exact purpose of distracting us so that they can control our attention—through bright colors, dopamine hits, and gamification. They are engineered for the sole purpose of seducing us into chasing and avoiding. The longer we stay in the app, the longer they keep us in the worthless cycle and the more money they can make from selling our attention to advertisers. When we give our attention to and spend our time in apps that only take from us and give nothing in return, we are reinforcing worthlessness.

To prevent this and move into the worthy cycle, Tammy needed to set healthier boundaries with herself, with her apps, and with her screen time so that she only engaged when she received fair compensation. This needed to be determined app by app and almost moment by moment. Instead of squandering her attention, she started to protect what was rightfully hers. She set aside a dedicated time for checking her apps, with a clear expectation of what she wanted in return for that time. When she used the apps, she wanted to feel hopeful and appreciated. Yet most often, she'd end up feeling hollow and anxious. Her new boundary was if she spent time on an app and felt worse, she deleted it. This helped her figure out which apps tended to be a waste of time and which apps might lead to an actual relationship.

"It's amazing how different I feel now with these apps. Rather than feeling like I'm constantly reacting to them, I feel calmer, like I have more control over myself. I'm not getting the same high from it, but I'm also not getting the same lows. More than anything, I think it's showing me that I just want to meet someone in real life. I don't want it to feel like I'm shopping online for a person. I'd rather sit down and have a conversation with someone." Tammy had been mindlessly using apps to avoid her feelings of rejection and chase her fantasy of finding the one. By enforcing healthy boundaries, she moved herself into the worthy cycle.

REAL STORIES: STACEY

Stacey, a highly organized sales executive and mother of two teenagers, was a self-proclaimed perfectionist. She shared, "I'm Type A to a tee. I can never sit still, I'm highly caffeinated, and I'm constantly on the go." Yet when asked what motivated her, she said, "It's not like I want to be this way. I'm exhausted all the time. But I don't know how to relax." She laughed. "Relaxing is so stressful! The minute I sit down, I berate myself for being lazy. My biggest fear is that I'll turn into a loser."

When Stacey shared her screen time photo, she said that she wasn't surprised by where her time was spent. She said that she's not really into social media and barely uses her phone other than for texting. She was, however, amazed to see how much time she spent texting. She said, "At first, I thought this must be an error, so I started scrolling through my texts to see how many I had sent today. Then I kept scrolling, and I kept scrolling, and I thought, 'Oh no.' I'm spending several hours a day texting. How is that even possible?"

When I asked if she felt like this amount of time was reinforcing worthiness or worthlessness, she said, "Honestly, I don't even know. It's like I'm just running around putting out fires and responding to whatever comes up next."

I told her, "You are not alone here. So many of us spend an unexpected amount of time on texting, emailing, or some other way of messaging. Most of us have an almost Pavlovian response to hearing a text chime or the notification of an incoming message. Every interruption, whether it's during your workday, your resting time, your commute, or while you're in line at the post office, costs you valuable resources: time, energy, focus, and attention."

Stacey's fear of being lazy had steered her toward overcompensating and overdelivering. Instead of caring for her true self, she mindlessly reacted to whatever demanded her attention. To move into the worthy cycle, she'd need to interrupt the pattern. The first step was to help safeguard her boundaries by silencing notifications so that she was the one determining when she picked up her phone, rather than being unconsciously reactive to the demands of her phone. The next step was to determine what she expected in return for the time spent texting.

She said, "I guess I expect to have stronger relationships. I want to be available for the people I love, so I always respond right away. But in the end, I feel like I'm just having a dumbed down conversation with my phone and less of a relationship with the people who matter."

Worthiness requires awareness. Rather than putting out fires out of a fear of appearing lazy, Stacey needed to honor what she truly wanted: more intimacy in her relationships. Her challenge was to find a way to be available without losing sight of what she really wanted. The following week, she shared, "Yesterday, I picked up my phone and called my son rather than sending a text. It felt so good to hear his voice. I always thought that texting was more efficient, but in just a few minutes, we got everything sorted out over the phone. He even said 'I love you' at the end of the conversation. That would have never happened over text."

YOUR WORTHY WORK

Very important: Under no circumstances are you allowed to do this exercise with the intention of self-shaming, adding to your to-do list, or causing yourself overwhelming shame spirals or anxiety. This exercise is only to be done with compassion and love.

Now it's your turn. Take a look at the photo of your screen time. Do you see any evidence that you might be chasing and avoiding? Do you see any evidence of lost time, hours or minutes that you can't really account for? Do you see any evidence of behavior that might be fueling the worthless cycle?

Once you've taken a good look at your photo, the next step is to determine one small change that you can make today to help you stay aware without checking out. This might mean that you remove an app altogether or that you set up time restraints or reminders to help you stay aware. It might mean that you need to set better boundaries with yourself and with others.

Our devices are not only interrupting our work but also our dinners, our conversations, and our sleep, and they are deteriorating the quality of our communication and connection with one another. When it comes to screen time, we are terminally settling for less than we deserve. All this distraction is taking a toll on our relationships, attention, physical health, and mental health.

To move into the worthy cycle, you'll need boundaries around what you're willing to give and what you expect in return. Here are a few boundaries to consider:

1. Only keep an app on your phone if it consistently reinforces worthiness. Remove all others.
2. Silence all notifications to stop distractions so that you protect the valuable asset of your attention.
3. Be conscious and deliberate about your engagement with your device rather than carelessly giving away your precious resources of time, attention, and energy.
4. Don't settle for dumbed down digital conversations. Intimacy and connection are crucial

resources that help build self-worth. Invest in the relationships that are most valuable to you by giving and receiving connection through real conversation.

5. Set times for digital silence and allow yourself time to restore.

6. Any time you find yourself going down a digital rabbit hole, gently bring your attention back to your true self, check in with your emotions, and get yourself back into the worthy cycle.

JOURNAL PROMPTS

1. What is your relationship to fear? Shame-guilt? Anger? Sadness?

2. Were your emotions honored and respected as a child? What were the messages you learned from your parents about your emotions?

3. When you want to turn off your emotions or numb emotional pain, what do you typically reach for?

4. Do you have any habitual chasing or avoiding behaviors that you would like to change? If so, what emotion would you need to embrace the most?

CHAPTER 6

Allowing and Owning

When I was about twenty-four years old, I was given a large cabinet television. Even way back in the old days of the '90s, it was an outdated relic, not a vintage, hipster, retro type of thing. I believe in its heyday owning such a thing was probably a mark of wealth, but by the time I received this monstrosity, it was more like something that you'd see forgotten and left behind after a flea market.

So let me paint you a picture of what was going on in my life right about the time I ended up with this beast of a gift taking up half my living room. For starters, my mom had just died from cancer. She was young (forty-four), and she went quickly and suddenly—nine weeks between the day that I'd found out she was sick to the day she died. I can't even say that

I was grieving; I was shocked and hollow and barely breathing. I was a ghost walking underwater. I mean, I was still me. I could smile and be charming, and I could laugh and be funny, but the real me was far away, deeply buried, and traumatized. It would be almost ten years before I began to process what had happened between my mother and me, let alone come to terms with her sudden death.

And yet life kept going. Bills needed to be paid, the dishes needed to be washed, and even the dust, relentless as it was, continued to collect on the surfaces of my home.

At the time, I'd just graduated from college, and I made the bulk of my income from teaching piano. This got me through school, paid well, and filled me with a sense of purpose. I loved my students, and over the years, I'd grown close to them and their families. Sometimes, I'd travel and teach at students' houses, and sometimes they'd come to mine. My simple living room—two love seats, a coffee table, an overflowing bookshelf, and a brick fireplace—became a sort of waiting room for parents while I taught their children.

It was at the end of one of these lessons that Barbara, one of my student's mothers, offered me a TV. Barbara was a friendly, modest, and soft-spoken attorney. She was in the process of remodeling their home, and they had just bought a new, modern (a.k.a. *smaller*) TV for their den. She noticed I didn't happen to have a TV and offered me their hand-me-down. I remember that she spoke of its hardwood exterior, its fine quality, and how it had been the top of the line at some point in time.

I don't remember exactly what she said, but I do remember what the conversation felt like. I remember wanting to please her, wanting to show appreciation for her generous offer, feeling like I needed to acknowledge the idea that she was giving me something highly valuable. I remember feeling like I was stuck behind a plastic mask of graciousness. And this is where I felt most at home, pretending to want things I didn't want and pretending to be grateful for the pain in the ass it created for me. I also remember feeling utterly trapped in a situation that I didn't want to be in and that this whole interaction didn't feel like an opportunity or a gift; it felt like obligation, guilt, and indebtedness. It felt like I had been trapped into owing something that I didn't want to owe. It felt like I had been given an ultimatum: either look like a self-important jerk or take the damned television.

So let's pause here, because I want to slow down this exact moment to highlight what was going on. The truth was I really didn't want any TV, let alone that one. At that point in my life, I had a very active social life, and I was almost never home in the evenings. I also lived in a rural area where there wasn't public access to television stations, so to make the TV usable, I'd have to add a monthly cable bill to my overhead. I had a small living room that was humbly decorated in a way that I loved. To absorb another thing into the room would mean that I'd probably have to rearrange my furniture or give up something of my own. In addition, I had no idea just how large, heavy, and overbearing this gift really was.

Rather than even taking a beat to check in with myself,

I reactively saw this hand-me-down as a gift of kindness that had to not only be accepted but earned. My own feelings and desires about the object were completely irrelevant. The only thing that mattered was to stay in good graces with someone who had shown me the tiniest bit of affection. This knee-jerk reaction was unconscious and blindingly overpowering. I was young, I had just lost my mother, and here was a mother figure offering me something. I couldn't say no, nor could I accept the gift without repayment. To do so would have been too vulnerable, too risky. What kind of selfish and ungrateful child declines kindness from her mother? What kind of selfish and ungrateful person accepts kindness without immediate reciprocation? I couldn't handle that type of imbalance. But I wasn't aware of my irrational logic, and it didn't take me more than a second to come up with a plan to repay the gifted debt.

Of course, none of this obligation was implicit in Barbara's offer, nor did my reaction have anything to do with her. This was solely my own projection; Barbara was simply the blank screen where I happened to be playing out old childhood wounds. Growing up, I had a keen understanding of how kindness, love, and care were used as leverage against me. I'd grown up in an atmosphere where nothing was given freely and everything had strings attached. To receive anything—food, a hug, a smile—without immediate reciprocation was to put myself at risk for punishment. I spent most of my childhood trying to erase my needs to soothe this imbalance of power. If I needed nothing, I felt safer. If I accepted nothing, I would owe nothing. This gave me the illusion of control—specifically that I could control the flow of what I'd understood to be love. This gave me the illusion of safety—meaning that if I always paid the imposed debt, I'd be able to avoid impending punishment.

Over twenty years later, I can see through the blind spot a little more clearly. And even though this TV scene seems ludicrous, it's a snapshot of something that I did time and time again. Whenever I was offered something that I didn't think I deserved, I contrived a way to go into debt. Through this self-imposed debt, I'd try to make myself an asset in hopes of preventing someone from leaving, abandoning, or hurting me. This debt gave me the illusion of control, where I was in charge of the balance of power. This debt also kept me stuck in the worthless cycle.

In hindsight, I'm pretty damned sure that Barbara wasn't trying to trap me into some bizarre web of debt. She simply needed to offload a TV. If I'd said no, she would have called the Salvation Army to come get it, or maybe the TV would have ended up at the dump. I highly doubt that she intended for any strings to be attached. Most likely, she saw a young adult who might benefit from her hand-me-down.

Barbara wasn't my mother, and she wasn't testing me. But this happened decades before my worthy work, and I was still operating from the idea that if I accepted more than I had earned, I would be made to pay. Selfishness wouldn't go unpunished.

This is how I ended up saying yes to the TV. This is why I drove a truck to her home to pick it up and rearranged my furniture to make space for the colossal piece of outdated technology. To make extra sure that I didn't appear ungrateful, I also installed cable service in my home. But I didn't just stop there; the imbalance was so uncomfortable for me that I had to go further. So I offered to teach Barbara's daughter for free, in exchange for what I deemed the TV's value to be. I can't remember how many months I offered for free, nor can I remember how I figured out what I thought the TV was worth. What I do remember was the desperation behind not wanting to be beholden, not wanting to be owned. I needed to make sure she knew that I would pay her back. I needed to make sure that I didn't receive anything more than I felt I deserved. So I gave away lessons that I couldn't afford to give.

I also remember Barbara's face, because this is a face that I saw many times throughout my life. When I offered the exchange of free piano lessons, she took a step away from me, like she didn't quite understand what I was doing. It was a look of disbelief, of confusion, probably even of insult. Through my eyes at the time, I was so eager to earn respect and love, I thought I was doing the right thing. I thought I was honoring her gift and that I was making myself appear more likable. I just wanted to even the score. I didn't want to be punished. I didn't want to lose her. I just wanted to repay the debt so that she'd continue liking me.

It would be decades before I understood what happened in that exchange. In hindsight, I can see Barbara's face along with the faces of so many other people throughout my life. People who simply wanted to help me or offer me something. But I couldn't allow it, couldn't handle it, couldn't even believe in it. All that kindness had to be returned quickly. I couldn't let it land on me. The minute I saw sweetness and generosity coming my way, I'd duck and cover and bounce it right back. This is how I continued to feel safe—I would control the flow to me and make sure there were never strings attached. I would not only underearn and overgive, I would make sure to never allow more than I deserved, and anything extra would always be repaid with interest.

You can imagine how fun it was to be in a relationship with me. *Oh, you brought me a flower? Here are ten flowers for you. Oh, you want to take me out to dinner? Here are five casseroles in return. Just put one in the oven at three fifty, and freeze the rest for a rainy day.* This is how I survived my childhood, and this tactic works well when you're living with mental illness, alcoholism, abuse, or any other terrible dysfunction. This strategy kept me alive, and it helped me feel a tiny bit of empowerment in an atmosphere of chaos and violence. But out there in the real world, this strategy just pushes good and loving people further away while leaving a wide-open door for the ones who want to exploit you. It makes you incredibly difficult to love and very easy to use. It's an impassible barrier for intimacy and a perfect recipe for worthlessness. Over years and decades, this strategy isolates you, preventing you from experiencing the benefits and risks of what it means to be human.

For me, it made love an impossible dream, one that I'd long ago deemed the stuff of fiction. Instead, I settled on a cheap substitute: admiration. If I couldn't be loved, I'd be admired. I'd make myself an asset, and I'd erase my own needs. I'd ignore my feelings, my desires, myself, and instead I'd keep selling the ideal version of myself—the one who needed nothing, the one who handled everything. That ideal self? She was the star who needed nothing. And the true me? She was the nothing who needed everything.

CONTRIVED DEBT

Maybe you have never accepted an antique TV, and maybe you've never offered to work for free in exchange for something that you didn't even want in the first place. And maybe you would have never gone so far as to add cable to your stack of monthly bills. But if you look closely at your life, I suspect you'll find places where you've invented debt without even realizing it. Places where you've contrived a way to pay back something that wasn't ever owed, nor could ever be repaid. Places where you decided that you didn't deserve what you received. Places where you created debt out of thin air to alleviate the discomfort of being given more than you could reconcile.

Maybe this looks like inviting your neighbors to dinner because they took out your trash while you were gone. Or maybe this looks like sending a thank-you note after receiving a gift. Or maybe this looks like bringing coffee to someone you accidentally wronged. In fact, many social niceties and general forms of politeness are often a reaction to an invented debt.

To be clear, there is nothing wrong with being polite or wanting to say thank you for a kindness received. In fact, gratitude reinforces worthiness. However, we get into trouble when, instead of being grateful, we try to pay back, control, or deflect.

Instead of allowing goodness to come our way, we contrive a way to bounce the goodness away. To be truly grateful means that you have to allow yourself the experience of what you're being offered. It means that you allow yourself to own what you've been given.

> *To be truly grateful means that you have to allow yourself the experience of what you're being offered.*

For example, how many times have you deflected a compliment? Someone tells you that you have a great smile, pretty hair, or kind eyes, and you wave your hand across your face as if batting away a fly. Or maybe you force out a quick *thank you*, but it makes you feel all itchy and squirmy until you gush some flattery back in their direction. Or maybe you counter the compliment by undermining it. Instead of saying "Thank you," you give a reason for not deserving the compliment in the first place. "What, this old thing?" or "You should see my sister's hair!" or "Well, after six thousand dollars of braces, my smile better be pretty." This is a sneaky strategy, and most likely you're not even aware of when or how often you do it.

Or maybe you feel terribly guilty for being given something. Maybe you feel like you received more than your fair share of intelligence, beauty, money, or privilege. Maybe you think it's unfair that you have the advantages you have or that you were given the personality or the loving parents you have.

So before we go on, I have to state an uncomfortable truth: Life isn't fair. It's never going to be fair. It's not possible to make it fair. And yes, some of us have been given more than our fair share. Some of us have been more lucky, more loved, more healthy than others. Some of us have been given a more symmetrical face, more athleticism, more intelligence, more access to clean water, more protection from abuse.

And none of this is fair.

When I spoke about earning, I talked about fair compensation as receiving what you rightfully deserve. This concept is important so that you can set boundaries with yourself and others around *under*earning. This concept of fairness is really about the low end of the spectrum, the bottom end of the receiving boundary.

This chapter is about allowing yourself to receive more than you think you deserve when more is given to you. It's about the top end of receiving. The upper limit of this boundary is infinity—meaning that you deserve infinite kindness, infinite love, infinite goodness. I want to make sure to clarify this, because if you gloss over this idea, it can almost sound like I'm an advocate for entitlement. That's not at all what I'm teaching here. Allowing yourself to own and appreciate benevolence is not entitlement. Entitlement is thinking that you deserve more than others; that's grandiosity, not self-worth. Entitlement isn't fair compensation. It is unethical, it deteriorates social bonds, and it reinforces worthlessness. When you lie, cheat, steal, or exploit, you not only degrade your self-worth, you additionally hurt those around you.

> *You deserve infinite kindness, infinite love, infinite goodness.*

This chapter isn't about thinking that you deserve more than others. It's about believing that we all equally deserve more than we can even imagine. It's about allowing yourself to inhabit, own, experience, and love what has been given to you. It's about understanding that sometimes you simply cannot earn what you've been given, nor should you try. And some of our most precious assets will never come from our direct efforts. They only come as gifts from God, the universe, people who love us, the angels, the fairy godmothers, or simply by a stroke of luck. I mean, how can one actually deserve a butterfly, a sunset, autumn leaves, or a starry night? You build self-worth by allowing yourself these gifts and taking full ownership of them. You reinforce worthiness by living in a state of gratitude.

However, trying to contrive a debt or control fairness by disregarding what you've been given only creates enormous amounts of suffering and ultimately keeps you stuck in the worthless cycle. This is the most common source of contrived debt, and the invented payment is typically a type of emotional suffering called toxic guilt. Where guilt is about repairing social connections, toxic guilt is about trying to gain control.

It works like this: It's not fair that I'm paid more than Alex, so in exchange, I feel guilty. Or it's not fair that I was born to middle-class parents who put me through college, so in exchange, I feel guilty. It's not fair that I'm taller, thinner, smarter, so in exchange, I feel guilty. Toxic guilt is a contrived way to pay off a debt that can never be paid. It's an attempt to control the uncontrollable. It's a way to try to even the score in a game that doesn't exist. It's a way to keep yourself from the benevolence that you've been given. It's a way of not having to take responsibility for what you've been given and instead levying an emotional tax in its place. By disregarding and disrespecting what's been given to you, you do not build self-worth; you simply reinforce worthlessness.

You cannot create equality, fairness, or justice through toxic guilt. You cannot solve the problems of social justice, privilege, ignorance, or prejudice through toxic guilt. If you want to make this world a better place, you must be willing to own what you've been given and use it to help others who haven't been given the same things. You must be willing to own it even if the unfairness is tipped in your favor—*especially* if the unfairness is tipped in your favor. And this can be radically uncomfortable, because sometimes this puts you face-to-face with the truth of just how unfair life is. Yet when you allow yourself to stand with a strong backbone and a wide-open heart, in the place of allowing and owning what you've been given, you see that you have infinite worth, as does everyone around you. You make no distinction, because there is no shortage of worth—everyone belongs, everyone is worthy, and everyone deserves. From this worthy place, you can affect true change. From this place, you take action to serve others, help right any wrongs, and help protect the marginalized. But when you're stuck in toxic guilt—trying to repay your privilege through suffering—you don't reinforce someone else's worthiness. You only reinforce your own worthlessness.

To move into the worthy cycle, you must give yourself permission to experience what you have been given. This isn't about being #grateful or #blessed. This is about fully inhabiting your life. It's about allowing kindness in. Allowing yourself to be seen, to be held, to be loved and cared for. This means that you take what you've been given and smile at the heavens and say thank you. It means that you take ownership of your life, your time, your energy, your infinite worth, and drink it all in.

INVISIBLE HANDS

In class, I give my students an assignment to help them become more aware of allowing and owning. I ask them to make a list of ways they've been supported, experiences they've been provided, gifts they've been given, and good fortune they did not earn, nor could they have ever earned. From a place of humility, I ask them to allow themselves full ownership of how they've been helped, what they've been given, and how their lives have been shaped by people they may have never even met and forces they may never understand.

Often, students turn this into a gratitude list, and this exercise is about something different, so let me explain. Gratitude is a beautiful quality; it's about being appreciative and thankful, a necessary component of worthiness. The difference here is that gratitude is something you feel—an adjective. Allowing and owning are something you do—verbs. This exercise is about the verbs, about the action of allowing—letting yourself have and giving yourself permission to experience. It's about the action of owning—laying claim, possessing, having and holding as your own. It's about noticing how the universe has conspired to smother you with love and about opening your arms to take it in without contriving a way to pay back that debt.

Think of it this way: you can be grateful to see a bowl of beautiful apples on the table—they are pretty, and they may brighten up your kitchen. But that doesn't mean that you've allowed yourself to touch one or that you've given yourself permission to eat one. So this exercise is about going further than gratitude; it's about inhabiting and expanding the idea of being thankful to the point that you completely allow yourself to possess, experience, and enjoy what you've been given. To acknowledge that you did not earn these things and to recognize that you do not owe anyone or anything in return. The mantra for this exercise is *I am worthy of this. I have always been worthy of this.*

For example, you might look back on your college years and see how many times the universe conspired to keep you safe. You left the party early. You didn't get into that car. You didn't go home with that guy. You might remember a feeling of being steered away from danger, or maybe that was the evening when you just couldn't find your keys. Regardless of the details, you know that you were kept out of danger and protected in ways that you couldn't have recognized at that time. So yes, be thankful for this, and have gratitude that the gods were watching over you. And then go further. Allow yourself to completely own the kindness. Open yourself to the miracles that benefited you. And then acknowledge that you are worthy of this. You are worthy of having the universe conspire in your favor. You are worthy of protection, even if you were young and made some not-so-great choices. You were always worthy.

Maybe you had an incredible mentor show up at the right moment in your life, and she saw something in you that you couldn't see in yourself. Maybe she made phone calls on your behalf, got you an internship with a friend of hers, or helped you fill out paperwork to land your first job. You might look back on this and just see it as dumb luck or being in the right place at the right time. And of course you're grateful for her and for everything that she did for you. And now, go deeper and allow yourself the gift, and fully own what you've been given. That means you acknowledge that you were worth her time, her attention, her help. You acknowledge that you were worthy of these gifts. You were then and you are now and you will always be. And everything that came from this experience is yours to own without any strings attached. You don't owe her, and you could never have earned what she did for you. And you are worthy of that. You were always worthy of everything she gave you.

Perhaps you look back on the immediate months after your divorce and see how support systems seemed to materialize to help you and your son find footing in your new home. When you look back on it, you don't remember asking for help or even reaching out to try to meet people. Instead, it was like people were called in by angels. Maybe you remember your neighbor showing up with lemonade on the day you moved in. Or you remember the mom at school who asked if you wanted to come over and talk. Maybe you remember that even the mailman, the people who delivered your furniture, or the landscapers who mowed your lawn all seemed to be keeping an eye out for you. You didn't earn this. You couldn't have earned this. Yet there they were, caring for you, caring for your son—and watching over you both. Maybe thinking about this brings tears to your eyes, and you want to write to each person and tell them thank you. It can be uncomfortable to recognize how much you were given, how many people helped through those painful months. And that's the point of this exercise. To open yourself to that discomfort and allow yourself to have these experiences, gifts, and love without trying to level the field. Instead of thanking them, stretch to see yourself as worthy of these gifts, to see your son was worthy of these gifts. You couldn't have done this alone. You were never meant to do this alone. You were worthy of the support and always will be.

Now think about your own life, and do this exercise yourself. Try to find at least ten examples. Across the top of the page, write *I am worthy of this. I have always been worthy of this.* List the miracles, the lucky breaks, the ways you've been helped. Notice where you couldn't have even tried to earn what you've been given. Notice where you wish you could pay back the cosmic debt, and instead allow yourself to have and hold what you've been given. You are part of the miracle called your life. And you are worthy of everything you've been given.

WORTHY WORK: HIDDEN MIRACLES

Take a picture of wherever you are in this moment, whether you're in your car eating lunch, at home on your couch, or outside on a hike. Just take a moment to capture exactly what's in front of you in this moment. This chapter is about expanding your awareness and allowing yourself to own the miraculous ways that life has conspired in your favor. You don't need to find a beautiful scene, go out into nature, or take a picture of something special. The more ordinary the time and place, the greater the opportunity to change your perspective. Just take a picture of whatever's in front of you right here, right now.

When I'm looking at student photos, I'm not necessarily looking at the subject of the picture. I'm looking for the student's ability to find the miraculous nature of their own worthiness in an everyday setting. I'm looking for how they interpret what they see and how they tell the story of what they see. It could be a picture of a parking lot, a baby's nursery, or a hospital waiting room. It could be a majestic sunset or a cluttered dining room table. No matter the scene, there is an infinite amount of worthiness available to be acknowledged, allowed, and owned.

This photo assignment is different from the previous

assignments. It isn't about a makeover or about taking action to reinforce worthiness. The first part of the assignment is to simply describe what you see in the photo in the way that you'd normally see it. To give you an idea of how this works, let me share a few examples.

REAL STORIES: AMY

Amy, a nurse at a busy New England pediatric hospital, signed up for my class to help her find more peace around her body size. A few years earlier, she'd had surgery that had left her bedridden for a few months. "During this time," she said, "I gained quite a bit of weight. There was nothing I could do but lie there in bed and watch TV. And I was okay with that, but now, a few years later, I can't seem to lose the weight." She shared that she can't look in the mirror without feeling ashamed and that other than her scrubs at work, she tends to only wear sweatpants. "I'd like to feel good, no matter what size I am. I want to be proud of my body for recovering. But the truth is, I'm not. I'm ashamed and disappointed that this has happened."

Amy's photo assignment showed a white car parked in a rainy parking lot. It looked like a strip mall with a deli, a market, and a UPS store. Amy shared, "I took this picture because of the white car. You can't see inside the car because of the rain, but inside are four young women. I watched them leave the market. They were all laughing. They looked like they were dressed for a photo shoot. Each of them had perfect hair, a perfect body, perfect clothes. I took this picture because I knew I needed to change my perspective here. The minute

I saw them, I wanted to roll my eyes and put my nose up in the air. I'd just come from work, and I was tired. It was as if I wanted to look down on their undeserved happiness. As if I'm better than them. The truth is, I felt envious. I immediately wanted to make excuses for why they are so happy—they're young, they don't have any responsibilities, they're thin. And then I stopped myself and took the photo right then."

Amy's story is a perfect example of how a lack of self-worth can color what we see and the story we tell ourselves. The women in the white car fueled Amy's worthless story and kept her in the worthless cycle. Rather than seeing the women as equal to her, she saw them as having something extra, something she couldn't have. She didn't celebrate them; she envied them. Rather than being happy to see joyful people, she justified her own unhappiness and looked down on them.

The next part of the assignment is an internal shift in the way that you witness what is around you. It's about shifting the way you see things and slanting it toward the staggering mystery and magic that life wants to offer you. It's about finding the unending ways that life offers to reinforce your worthiness and then describing the scene from that point of view.

I asked Amy, "How is this scene conspiring in your favor? What miracles do you need to allow and own here?"

She said, "I don't even know where to start. I look at that white car, and I just feel old and fat. I'm not seeing any miracles here."

"What else is in the photo? Try to focus on something else."

"Well, there's a UPS store in the picture, and that's pretty amazing. I mean, you can box something up and send it any-where in the world. I don't have to drive the box around by myself. I just hand it off and know that it will get to where I want it to go. I know you pay for that, but it's really amazing that I can pay such a small fee for something to go halfway around the world."

With that small shift, she began to see other things within the photo. It was raining, and their community needed the rain; it had been a dry spring. She didn't earn the rain. She didn't build the parking lot, yet it was there for her convenience. She loved that market and would stop there after work anytime she needed something. Someone else stocked those shelves, and she was benefiting from that person's efforts. She was able to pick up some tea for the morning. When she finally got to rewriting the story of the women, the entire scene had opened up for her.

"These women were happy. They smiled at me as they passed me. They were laughing and jumping in the puddles. They weren't taking themselves seriously. They were having fun. They were beautiful and joyful, and it was a true gift to be able to witness them. To remember that I could also get out and enjoy the rain. That I could smile for no reason. Instead of needing to put them down, I see that they are worthy of their joy, and so am I."

By changing the story and allowing herself the gifts in that scene, Amy moved out of the worthless cycle, where she fil-tered the scene through her ideal image, and into the worthy cycle, where she observed the scene through the lens of her true self. Rather than shielding herself from the joy, she celebrated their joy. Rather than feeling envious of their youth, she embraced their playfulness. Rather than rolling her eyes and trying to maintain her superiority, she saw them as an invitation to allow herself some lightheartedness.

"I can't believe how different I feel," Amy said. "This picture held so much shame for me and seemed to highlight everything that was wrong with me. And now, it's the opposite. It makes me want to go outside and play in the rain."

REAL STORIES: HEATHER

Another student, Heather, an avid gardener in the Pacific Northwest, signed up for my class just for fun. Her kids were both in college, and she was looking to enrich her life with new experiences. Years ago, she built a small flower shack at the end of her driveway for her kids to sell flowers from the garden. What was once a flower shack had become a community farm stand where everyone from the neighborhood could share from their gardens and take what they needed. She shared, "It's my way to connect with the people around me. I love working in my garden, and I love to share what I've helped create."

When Heather shared her photo assignment, she said, "I have to admit, since the minute we were given this assignment, I haven't seen anything in the same way. I thought about sharing a picture of my garden, but that almost seemed too easy. Obviously I work hard in my garden, but the fact that plants grow and flowers bloom? That's always been a miracle to me. Last night, I sat on my couch knowing I needed to post something, so I took a picture of what was right there in front of me: my bookcase."

Her photo showed an overflowing bookcase. Books were stacked horizontally, vertically, diagonally. Well worn and cherished, she had rows of classics—Dostoevsky, Hawthorne, Steinbeck, Austen. There were slim bound books of poetry—Heaney, Bly, and Oliver—one with a brown-and-white-spotted feather as a bookmark. There were piles of gardening books, bird watching guides, flower arranging manuals, and stacks of self-help books.

She said, "Before this assignment, I would have just seen my book collection as something that I had created over time. Some of the books were gifts, but most of them were chosen and purchased by me. In one way, I can see this bookcase as something that I've earned. I've spent my money on collecting these books. I've spent my time reading them. But this assignment opened me up to seeing it in a different way. It seems obvious now, but I hadn't considered that I haven't written a single word. I purchased the books, but I didn't write them. Each one of these books has touched my life, changed me, and taught me something. They influenced my life and the lives of everyone close to me. How could I ever try to earn someone else writing down their wisdom or their story? It's not possible to earn it, nor could I ever return the favor. These are gifts that have changed my life, page by page. When I look at my bookcase through the lens of this exercise, I can see that this bookcase holds more value and more knowledge than I could ever try to accumulate through my own effort. Each one of these books has been a gift for me."

REAL STORIES: TANYA

Tanya, a first-year resident, signed up for class in hopes of quieting her overactive inner critic. Throughout med school, she'd always been an outstanding student, but now, sleep deprived and weary, she seemed to constantly second-guess herself. She said, "I used to always know the answers. I never even thought about feeling confident. But now, outside the academic world, my self-doubt is paralyzing me. The longer I worry about something, the less I seem to know."

She shared, "The only place where my self-doubt seems to fade away is out on the trail. I try to run there a few times a week. So that's where I took my picture."

Her photo showed a dirt trail winding through a parklike setting. Tall green grass, bent with the wind, flanked each side of the trail. Long beards of Spanish moss hung from under a canopy of oaks. It was springtime, and the photo seemed to hum with life. Off to the side of the trail, there was a galvanized trash can. Other than that, the photo was simple and natural beauty.

Tanya shared, "I came upon this trash can today near the middle of my run. This section of the trail typically has quite a bit of picnic debris. It's beautiful and shady under the oaks, and I think a lot of people like to stop and hang out here. But there's always litter left behind. Candy wrappers, beer cans, plastic water bottles—things like that are just strewn around either through carelessness or by accident. I'm so used to it, I don't even notice it anymore. But today was different. As I passed through this section of trail, I noticed the trash can. That was new. And I also noticed the lack of trash on the ground. That was also new. But the reason I took this picture was because of the sign."

I zoomed into the picture and then saw it: a homemade wooden sign fastened to the trash can. In hot-pink paint, looking as if it was painted by a child, it read *Please don't litter.*

Tanya said, "I almost wept when I saw it. Here I was, out on a trail that I dearly love, passing through a section that's always covered with trash. And someone else took it upon themselves to bring a garbage can out here and make a handwritten sign. It's overwhelming and beautiful. I did not ask for them to do this, yet I am benefiting from it. I've passed through this section dozens of times and never even thought about what could be done. Yet someone else had a vision and went through the effort to care for this land. Typically, I would have tried to avoid noticing the depth of this kindness. It would have made me feel guilty, like I should have done it. But I realized today that I am worthy of having someone else clean this for me. We are all worthy of that."

YOUR WORTHY WORK

Very important: Under no circumstances are you allowed to do this exercise with the intention of self-shaming, adding to your to-do list, or causing yourself overwhelming shame spirals or anxiety. This exercise is only to be done with compassion and love.

Now it's your turn. Take a picture of wherever you are in this moment. The more ordinary the time and place, the greater the opportunity to change your perspective. Just take a picture of whatever's in front of you right here, right now.

Simply describe what you see in the photo in the way that you'd normally see it. Maybe you see it through the lens of your ideal image, or maybe you wouldn't typically even pay attention to the details held within the scene. Write a few sentences describing how you'd see the contents of this photo on an average day.

Now shift your perspective. Through the lens of your true self, allow yourself to witness the gifts within the scene. Ask yourself: How is this scene conspiring in my favor? What miracles do I need to allow myself to own here? How is this scene reinforcing my own worthiness? Write a few sentences describing the scene from this new point of view.

JOURNAL PROMPTS

1. How do you react when someone gives you a compliment or a gift or does a favor for you?
2. What is the greatest gift you've ever received?

3. How do you react when you receive more than you feel you deserve?

4. What do you most need to allow into your life?

5. What do you most need to own about where you are right now?

Afterword

I used to think I was self-made. The story I used to tell was one of rising out of a childhood of abuse, putting myself through college, starting my first business in my midtwenties, and bootstrapping my way through life. This is how I *had* to tell the story, because I couldn't wrap my mind around anything else. Nothing could be owned unless it was earned, and therefore everything had been earned by me alone. This was the story, the rise of the ideal image, that fueled my worthless cycle. I'd go around and around this story, always hoping to prop myself up on a pedestal of worthiness, never understanding how arrogant, how naive, and how ridiculous it was to take credit for my life as if I alone were the playwright, the protagonist, and the audience. In this story, my successes were accomplished on my own, and any failures were chalked up to injustice. In this story, I was a single mother doing it all! I was an entrepreneur making it happen! I'd been on Oprah, for god's sake—modern-day proof that I was, indeed, somebody!

The issue with this story, beyond the glaring problem of reality, was that underneath it was simply a woman desperate for love, acceptance, and belonging. And the more I went up to the mountaintop to try to proclaim my worth, the lower I dropped into a debilitating sinkhole of worthlessness.

This was what I had to reconcile if I was ever going to be able to climb my way out of that hole. This would have to stop if I was ever going to be able to hold on to some sense of self-worth. I would have to come to terms with myself, my story, and my life in a radically different way. And this was terrifying for me, because I felt lower than low, emotionally bankrupt, and so afraid of feeling even worse about myself. So I'd just try harder, give more, and then pat myself on the back for being such a hard worker. I'd refuse help, disregard kindness, and give myself accolades for how self-reliant I'd been. I look back on myself at this time with nothing but compassion for the woman who thought that this was the only way forward. I wasn't trying to be arrogant or to push people away. I was completely ignorant and unaware of what I was doing. To me, it felt like I simply had to keep myself from drowning. And the only thing keeping me above water was my heroic story. I didn't realize that this story was never going to save me. Instead, it was more like concrete blocks tied to my waist, pulling me under faster than I could ever swim. It was a terrible and painful way to live. It was a life where everything was up to me. One where I was alone. One where I'd always be alone. It was a life lived in a tiny glass house with a very low ceiling. Everyone could see in, and no one could reach me there.

As I gained self-worth, cracks started to form in my hero story. As I began to see myself as worthy, I also began to see others as worthy. When I stopped focusing on myself as the leading lady, it was as if, out of the periphery, all the unrecognized participants began to appear onstage. The invisible hands who'd helped me along my path. The angels, the teachers, the friends, the loved ones who had always been there to help me, to guide me.

From a foundation of worthiness, I could now see that I was never alone. That there was kindness and goodness that had helped me every step of the way. Throughout my childhood, I had teachers who (in hindsight) seemed to be aware of what was happening at home. Teachers who gave me jobs after school, who told me of possible futures, who helped me see that I might be okay someday. I had friends who watched out for me, as did their parents. I was taken on a college tour completely funded by a classmate's grandmother, solely because she didn't want me to fall through the cracks.

My college tuition was almost entirely paid for by the invisible hands of another mother figure. I did not know this at the time—she anonymously sponsored many young women who wanted a college degree. She believed in women helping women. She not only paid my tuition but also gave me a job and helped me start my first business. She gave me access to people I would never have met otherwise. Most remarkably, she insisted that I play piano for a dinner that she hosted for

Benazir Bhutto, prime minister of Pakistan and the first woman to head a democratic government in a Muslim-majority nation. To be in a room with such a powerful woman, to play piano for her, to have a conversation with her—it changed my life. I did not earn that privilege; it was a gift from a woman who wanted me to see what strong women can do, and that experience is still a source of profound inspiration to this day.

Beyond college, there were countless hands that reached out from behind the scenes of my story. People all around me who helped me heal, grow, and learn. There was never a time when I was the sole hero of the story. My Oprah appearance was a gift from my teacher who had put in a good word for me. My experience of single motherhood was more of a village raising me while I raised my daughter. I think back on all the kind people who saw something in me and who took a risk on me. I think back on the people who offered me shelter when I needed it. Food when I was hungry. Kindness when I felt broken. None of this was by my own hand.

Once I began to see my life through these eyes, I was overwhelmed with humility, with thanks. Even the car that I drove became this miraculous piece of equipment that had been created by complete strangers far away. The food on my plate had been picked by hands in the fields not too far away from the home that I'd been allowed to live in. Rather than see everything through the eyes of what I had earned, I began to see everything that I had been given. Things that I couldn't earn. Things that I shouldn't ever try to earn.

The kindness of strangers. The stoplights that kept me safe

at an intersection. The movies that kept me entertained in the evenings. The coffee that made getting out of bed in the wee hours of the morning possible. I did not create these things. I did not make them happen. There were miracles upon miracles that were unfolding all around me. To realize this, to let this in, to allow myself the benevolence that had always surrounded me: this changed everything.

In the beginning of my worthy work, I did the same work that I've taught you in this book. I had to learn to set boundaries around my overspending and stop being reckless with myself, with my heart, with my time, energy, and money. I also had to learn how to require what I deserved, how to contain myself and wait, and how to walk away from situations that continually depleted me. By keeping myself in the worthy cycle, becoming aware of unconscious distractions, and deliberately choosing new actions, I began to change.

Where I was once driven by the hope of attaining an illusory feeling, I learned that worthiness wasn't somewhere that I could get to. It wasn't something that would land on me. It wasn't something that anyone else could give me. Worthiness is like a muscle, and the more I kept myself from overspending and underearning, the stronger I would become. I learned that worthiness is a state of mind and a way to metaphorically hold myself. It isn't an endgame; it is a process.

It was only after setting the foundation for worthiness that I could start to incorporate allowing and owning. To try to jump straight to gratitude, when you have no boundaries in place to support you, is simply a spiritual bypass—a defense mechanism that shields you from the truth—and this type of bypass keeps you in the worthless cycle. To build self-worth, you need to own your stories, your feelings, and your behavior. Over time, you build a connection with your true self, gaining pieces of yourself as you practice staying in the worthy cycle. To experience, allow, and own the gifts in your life, you must have a clear understanding of your true self, and this takes time, patience, and practice. This is why I save teaching this concept for the end, because without a strong foundation, you won't be able to break through that last glass ceiling of self-worth.

To build self-worth, you must first take responsibility for yourself. You must learn how to caretake your precious asset of self. But to truly feel, act, and live with an abiding sense of worthiness, you must then learn how to allow even more than you ever thought possible. Because the truth is, the most valuable things in your life cannot be earned, nor are they even deserved. Our most treasured memories, relationships, and moments unfold in an organic fashion, and we are simply invited to witness them, live them, breathe them in. Rather than turn away, you must learn to allow, care for, and own what has been given to you.

> *Because the truth is, the most valuable things in your life cannot be earned, nor are they even deserved.*

This process is personal, it happens within you, and it doesn't really provide any external evidence. Therefore, I'll simply share what this process was like for me.

For most of my life, I had thought that I needed to earn love. As I explained before, I thought that if I was always an asset and never a liability, I would be indispensable. This played out in my relationships with men over and over, where I became the fixer, the helper, the servant, the cheerleader, and asked for nothing other than to be tolerated.

The winter of the double-bagging team retreat was a major turning point in my life. I had overspent and underearned to the point of physical, financial, and emotional exhaustion. I had nothing left to give. My body was broken and healing, my business had been reduced to almost nothing, and I had no more earning power left within me.

I had already started to piece together a new story for my life, one where I didn't need to be the hero, the bootstrapper, the creator, the maker, the doer. One where I had instead inherited infinite gifts that amounted to more than I would ever earn on my own. One where I no longer had the energy to bat kindness away. One where I had no more reserves to take on contrived debt.

I knew that I had to learn how to go a different way. And maybe it would be terrible. And maybe it would lead me even further into worthlessness. At the time, I had no idea how it would play out. I just knew that I could no longer pretend that these patterns were working for me. I had hit rock bottom. If arrogance and self-reliance had taken me to that dead-end road, maybe I needed to take the opposite approach.

During this time, I'd also met a man—a good man, a caring man—and I'd fallen in love with him. Looking back on that winter, I can see so many gifts, so many opportunities for growth, and so many places where I had to surrender old patterns. When I think about that winter, I think about being wrapped in a blanket, drinking tea, and staring at the Pacific Ocean for hours. I don't remember talking as much as I remember the simple ease of being. I would come up against this involuntary compulsion to be entertaining, funny, a great storyteller, or dazzling in some way or another. And then I'd stop myself and just sit quietly and allow myself the view of the ocean. It was uncomfortable for me to do this. I felt like I was out of control. I could feel the old worthless story still coursing through my veins: *If you don't do something to earn it, he won't stay. If you don't perform, he won't love you. If you don't dazzle, he'll get bored.*

Trying not to do what I'd always done, I stopped myself from attempting to manage him, manage myself, our future. Yet I was deeply suspicious and couldn't really wrap my mind around someone who would just care about me for no reason at all. I couldn't be my superhero self, and he didn't need anything fixed for him. I was aware of my patterns, and I deliberately sat on my hands and white-knuckled myself through the compulsion of wanting to fall back into my old unworthy ways. If I wanted to change, I'd have to do something I'd never done before: I'd have to allow him to see me, know me, and care for me as is.

I was sick and recovering, I was broke, and life had given

me a hard beating. I didn't feel pretty. I didn't feel sexy. I didn't have access to the currency that I'd used in past relationships. I couldn't do anything to make this guy love me, to be indispensable to him, to make myself an asset. I had to just be who I was. Period.

I was more vulnerable and more humbled than I'd ever been. His kindness was like looking at the sun—it was painfully sharp and difficult to endure. Deep within me, I felt the knee-jerk response of wanting to shield myself against him. As if I might die from sweetness or from generosity. When it got too overwhelming, I'd go in another room, brace myself against a wall, and breathe slowly until I could feel my feet on the ground again, reminding myself that I would not die from this.

But I was wrong. There was a part of me that had to die, and all that terror, all that panic, and the shocking feeling of free fall was coming from the exact part of me that knew its life was being threatened.

I remember where I was when my ideal image died. And I remember what killed her.

Blake and I were lying on a trampoline, overlooking the mountains and the ocean. The sun was just warm enough to feel like a blanket protecting us against the cool marine air. We lay quietly, side by side, watching the clouds, the sea, the whales passing by for most of the afternoon. Every so often, we'd talk a little and then fall back into a peaceful and comfortable silence. There, on the trampoline, the grandeur, the magnificence, the incredible beauty of nature, of life—I couldn't keep it at bay. It was too powerful, too much.

We talked about how good it feels to be held, to be touched, and how the body craves this, needs this. He grabbed my hand and pulled me toward him. He wanted to hold me. He wanted me to lie on him. I didn't really understand what he was asking or why he would want this, but I could feel the danger in it. I was triggered and afraid and began to try to manage my fear. Without thinking, I rolled over to him and carefully positioned myself in a sort of hover above him. I pressed the tops of my feet into the trampoline, holding my lower body in a stiff horizontal position above his. My upper body was propped on one elbow as if peeling myself away from him. It was uncomfortable and awkward, like a plank position over another human being. I was sort of touching him and technically above him, and I thought it odd that this was what he wanted.

But then I saw something in his face. It was the same face that I'd seen time and time again. It was the same as Barbara's face and my old teacher's face. It was the look of disbelief, of worry, and maybe a look of insult, but mostly I saw compassion. Like he saw my fear, and he saw what I was doing, and even if he didn't understand why I was doing it, he was willing to be patient and figure it out with me. He didn't look away, and he didn't make it easier. He simply smiled and said, "No. I want you to lie on me."

In that moment, while hover-planking above a man on a trampoline, I had nowhere to go. My muscles shook from fatigue, and this was an impossible position to hold for much longer. But to relax and lie down would mean that he would experience the entire weight of me, all the pounds, the inches, and a lifetime of baggage. He would experience the real me, and I couldn't let that happen. I didn't want to lose him. I didn't want him to experience the full liability of me, the heaviness, the density of my pain, the burden of my neediness, the gravity of my worthlessness. So I stayed in my plank position, my body vibrating with exhaustion, and tears fell from my eyes onto his T-shirt.

"I can't," I sobbed. "I don't want you to find out how heavy I am."

It was the most honest thing I could say, even though I felt like a child saying it. Even though I knew it was irrational and impossible to explain. Even though I knew that within that truth, there was a larger truth that I had just confessed. My muscles were twitching and wanted so badly to go back to lying side by side. To save myself from the unbearable vulnerability of this moment.

Slowly, quietly, he steadied his gaze at me and said, "Lie on me. I want your weight on me."

My body shook from exhaustion, my feet ached, and my arms buckled. The harder I tried to push away from the trampoline, the more awkward the position became. Like being caught in a large web, nothing was solid and everything was moving. I was tired and sad and scared. The only way forward would be to make a choice right then and there: to do what I had always done or to choose to see myself as worthy of being held. Without earning anything, without helping anyone, without holding my body tight and stiff.

So I did the unimaginable. I closed my eyes and surrendered. Millimeter by millimeter, I slowly lowered myself, gasping through tears. The space between my body and his—it was vast, and it held a lifetime of information. I lowered my body down and then farther down. It was miles before I felt something solid, his chest, before I could feel his heartbeat, his breath, and I could feel mine. He was alive and holding all my weight, and I was still breathing.

To allow myself to be held. To allow the full weight of me to be supported by another human being. To own that moment and inhabit it fully. This wasn't about romance, and this wasn't about being saved by a knight in shining armor. I had no idea what would happen between Blake and me—that was yet to be written, and it wasn't even the point. This wasn't about him or us; it was about me. It was about realizing that all of it—all my pain, all my mistakes, all my wounds, this entire idea that I was a liability in the world, that I was a burden, that I had to earn and achieve and manage an image so that someone somewhere would deem me worthy—had been wrong. It was about learning that this heavy body, this life, this person was worthy of being held.

I was worthy.

I had always been worthy.

And I would always be worthy.

And this worth had nothing to do with what I gave, what I could do, or what I could accomplish. It had nothing to do with how I looked, how thin I was, or how pretty I was. It had nothing to do with my age, my intelligence, or my successes or failures.

It was like my entire life had been lived in that damned

plank position, and I had spent most of my life holding myself rigid, trying to prove my worthiness.

When all along, I just needed to let go and allow myself to be held.

And this is what life wants for you too. It wants you to recognize your patterns of worthlessness. It wants you to choose better stories. It wants you to deeply connect with your true self, your true desires, your true feelings. It wants you to set boundaries so that you take charge of underearning and overspending. It wants you to live with a strong backbone and an open heart.

Life wants to feel the full weight of you. It wants to hold you. It wants to protect you.

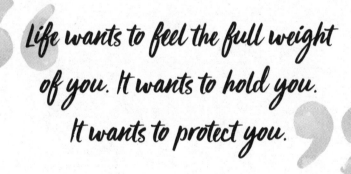

> Life wants to feel the full weight of you. It wants to hold you. It wants to protect you.

It wants you to let yourself be held—in all your glory and all your inadequacies and all the mystery and magic in between. And from this worthy place—when you allow yourself to be held in the gratitude and the wonder and the majesty of this beautiful existence—take ownership of this unbelievable privilege. Fully inhabit the honor, the respect, and the generosity of the experience that you've been given.

Let yourself be held within the miracle that is you and the miracles that are unfolding all around you.

Allow yourself to feel, act, and live with the deep and abiding knowledge that you are worthy.

Reading Group Guide

1. How did it feel to take the worthiness quiz at the end of the introduction? Were you surprised by your results? How did that quiz prepare you for the rest of the book?

2. The core of the worthless cycle is an unhealthy relationship with our ideal image. What's the difference between setting healthy goals and chasing an ideal image?

3. Did you participate in the worthy work challenges throughout the book? Which was the most difficult for you? Did you begin noticing themes in your responses?

4. Worthless stories are, by definition, out of sync with what we really want and feel. So where do they come from? Does the critical voice in your head sound like someone from your real life?

5. What worthy story will you use to kick-start the worthy cycle? Describe where you decided to start and why.

6. The author writes, "You gain self-worth by claiming more of your true self, not by thinking that you're awesome." What distinction is she making?

7. How do you move from recognizing your worthless voice's thoughts to interrupting them? What strategy works best for you to calm down the negativity and tune back into your true self?

8. When it comes to money, time, and attention, the author emphasizes that you can only spend from a place of excess. What obstacles prevent you from protecting your resources in this way?

9. What did you learn about yourself by thinking about social media use in terms of chasing and avoiding?

10. Name one small way and, if you can, one large way that you will change your life after reading *The Worthy Project*.

Acknowledgments

So much gratitude to my agent and advocate, Rebecca Gradinger; Sourcebooks; and my brilliant editor, Anna Michels, who helped refine this work for print. To Kerri Kolen and Audible, who gave the original green light for this project. To my husband, Blake, who taught me how to be held.

About the Author

Meadow DeVor is a self-development teacher with a modern approach to spirituality, money, and personal growth. Since 2007, she has led courses, trainings, and retreats both online and throughout the United States. She's the author of *Money Love: A Guide to Changing the Way You Think about Money* and has had the pleasure of being a guest on *The Oprah Winfrey Show*. She speaks, writes, and teaches extensively on how our relationship to life itself is an exact reflection of our deepest held beliefs about our own worth. She lives with her husband in Big Sur, California.